THE
DESSERT
SCENE

Toronto's Top Dessert Spots
Reveal Their Secret Recipes

Rose Reisman

PUBLISHED BY ROSE REISMAN

Copyright © 1988 by Rose Reisman

Canadian Cataloguing in Publication Data

Reisman, Rose, 1953-
   The Dessert Scene
Includes index
ISBN 0-9693365-0-0

1. Desserts 2. Restaurants, lunch rooms, etc.
 Ontario – Toronto I. Title
 TX 773. R44 1988   641.8'6   088-893315-1

Printed by Friesen Printers
Altona, Manitoba

Design: Don Fernley
Photography: Richard Allan
Props/food stylist: Susan Renouf
Editorial: Nancy Kilpatrick

Typeset by Menesetung Enterprises Incorporated
Toronto, Ontario, Canada

Printed in Canada

Inn on the Park (cover photo)
Cointreau Chocolate Decadence

DEDICATION

I dedicate this book to the man who has always supported each and every crazy endeavour that I have undertaken. In this project Sam was asked to sample literally hundreds of desserts—not an easy task. I believe that the extra pounds left with him indicate the success of this book. Also, without the daily assistance of Edel and Conchita, I could never have completed the book in the time I did. And last, but not least, the tiny helping hands of Natalie and David were crucial to this book's success.

Contents

BIOGRAPHY

Rose Reisman is a 34-year-old Toronto resident and dessert afficionado. A self-taught baker with over twelve years' experience, she holds two post-graduate degrees, an M.B.A. and an M.F.A, both from York University. Rose most recently taught business at Seneca College and lives in Toronto with her husband and two young children.

ACKNOWLEDGEMENTS

Fabrics in the photographs were given by B. B. Bargoon's.

All desserts in the photographs were specially prepared and decorated by the chefs who created them.

Introduction

For the past dozen years, baking has been—and remains—a love of mine. Over that period, I have become familiar with a vast number of the better and lesser-known recipe books, predictably ranging from the exceptional to the banal. Those exceptional few, in general, utilize ingredients, techniques, experience and capability which are outside the scope of all but the expert homemaker. Therein lies a major premise to this effort.

My idea was to prepare a dessert specialty book which melded the unrivalled talents of famous chefs with the skill base of the ordinary homemaker. When combined, the chef's talents and the homemaker's skills create an outstanding replica of the original. Perhaps a little bit like tracing over the work of a great artist like Chagall or Picasso and emerging with a more favourable result than one otherwise would.

I have threatened, seduced or bribed these remarkable chefs into divulging their most popular recipes and then transcribed each recipe into terms and technique a novice can understand and follow.

This was no easy task. Each of these recipes has been tested and re-tested, and altered, as required, in concert with the originating chef. The result I am very proud to display in this book. Each recipe is sophisticated in presentation and taste, yet remarkably straight-forward to prepare. At the beginning of the book, I have included basic hints and tips which will ensure even the neophyte a round of applause at dessert time.

So, at last, after much hard work, this is the result of the collaborative effort of master chefs and skilled homebaker. The recipes are easy to prepare, so let's collaborate now to produce these desserts, renowned for their excellence across this continent.

ROSE REISMAN

Helpful Hints
to Achieve Perfect Results
with the Following Recipes

Please, no matter how competent a baker you are, read this brief section carefully. It is well worth the time.

Chocolate Melting – Break into smaller pieces and melt in a microwave under defrost for 2-4 minutes, depending on the quantity. You can also use a double boiler over simmering heat. Transfer melted chocolate into new bowl and let cool slightly before adding eggs, whipping cream liquors, or whipped egg whites.

Curls – use a vegetable peeler or cheese slicer. Hold chocolate chunk in hands for a few minutes to soften. Peel chocolate turning it around in your hands when one side starts to melt. Store in a cool place.

Gelatin – one package equals one tablespoon gelatin (15 ml). It should be dissolved by first covering with cold water, approximately 1/4 cup (50 ml) Let this rest one minute, then add 1/4 cup hot water (50 ml). Stir until melted.

Layering Cakes – For cakes over two layers, frosting between layers is made easier if layers are placed in the border of a fitting springform pan and iced in the pan just before topping or sides are done. Place in freezer for a few minutes until set, remove springform pan and ice the tops and sides. This prevents the icing from sliding out the sides.

Testing Cakes for Doneness – All cakes give approximate baking times because all ovens, pans and measurements can differ. Therefore, ten minutes before the given recipe time is up, cakes should be tested by inserting a toothpick or tester into the middle. If wet, keep checking at 5-minute intervals. Sometimes a little bit of wetness in the middle will yield a moister cake.

Pecan Pies and Cheesecakes – These differ from other cakes because they need to be moist, so a small portion of the centre will remain loose.

Whipping Cream and Whipping Egg Whites – All cream and egg whites must be cold, fresh and whipped in clean, dry bowls in order to achieve the proper stiffness. If the bowl is wet or has any hint of foreign particles in it, then the cream and egg whites will never beat properly. Whip only until stiff peaks are reached. Over-beating cream will result in a curdled consistency.

Fresh and Frozen Fruit Purées – Usually 1 1/2 cups of fresh fruit (375 ml) will yield approximately 3/4 cup (175 ml) of purée, but always measure. When using frozen fruit, defrost and then be sure to strain the excess liquid before puréeing.

Food Processor – If a food processor is used to mix cakes or cookies, keep this in mind: after the flour has been added, use on-off motions to combine flour with other ingredients—gently. Avoid beating or the cake will be dry.

Molds – To invert, dip the bottom of the mold into a larger pan filled with boiling water for 5 seconds. Invert onto serving dish. If unsuccessful, try another 2-3 seconds. Note that the mold is kept in the water too long, the ingredients will melt.

Parchment Paper – The greatest non-stick paper ever invented. This paper can be bought in grocery stores or specialty cooking stores. It can also be reused. Butter and flour the paper to guarantee 100% success.

Garnishes

You don't have to be an expert pastry chef. Using basics can achieve spectacular results.

Icing or confectioner's sugar or cocoa – Sift over cake

Strawberries - Decorate with sliced strawberries.

Chocolate-glazed Strawberries – Melt chocolate with 1/2 tsp (2ml) of vegetable oil and dip half of strawberry with fork or toothpick into chocolate. Refrigerate until hardened on wax paper.

Jelly Glazes – Used to give fruit a sheen. Melt 2 tbsp (30 ml) and brush over fruit.

Nuts – Toast in oven on cookie sheet at 450° (230°) or in dry pot over high heat on stove, until golden brown. Grind into desired texture.

Chocolate Glaze (Ganache) – Chocolate glaze contains half as much whipping cream as chocolate. Melt chocolate. Add cream and blend. Usually 4 oz. of chocolate (125 ml) will glaze top of cake. Therefore use 2 oz. of cream (60 ml).

LIST OF NECESSARY AND/OR HELPFUL EQUIPMENT

Food processor – Great for grinding, beating and mixing. Do not use for whipping unless you have special attachment.

Electric beater – Use for whipping, creaming, beating or stirring. Gives greater volume to eggs, butter and sugar.

Springform Pans – small, medium and large are all good to have on hand.

Large cake pans - 8 to 9" (20-22cm.) round pans are useful, especially when lined with parchment paper.

Bundt or tube pans – Useful for pound or fruit cakes

Decorative mold pans (2-4 cup [500ml.-1 l.]) – good for mousses.

Jelly Roll Pans – useful for sponge recipes. Line with parchment paper.

Bain-marie – Large pan which is filled with water, into which baking pan is placed to give cake extra moisture. *Note*: Do not put springform pans into a Bain-Marie – they leak.

ANDRE SZILAGY

Right in the heart of Toronto's fashionable and exclusive Bay/Bloor area, just across the street from Creed's, one of the city's most exclusive women's clothing stores, is A Piece Of Cake. George Calb, owner and manager, has operated the café—which now serves food as well as desserts—for nine years. The clientèle tends to be the after-theatre and movie crowd.

Pastry Chef Andre Szilagy came to Toronto from Hungary and began working at the Queen Elizabeth Hotel. He later owned his own pastry shop but five years ago, decided to join A Piece Of Cake, which he had admired for years.

Andre creates about 40 different desserts, varying weekly. He says that customers seem to prefer chocolate mousse and cheesecakes plus an old-time favourite, strawberry shortcake.

From his large repertoire, Andre has carefully selected two desserts to share with you.

Peach Shortcake with Cream

Preheat oven to 350°F (180°C).
Line 10 x 15" jelly roll pan with buttered and floured parchment paper
(25 x 38 cm).

Cake

6 egg yolks $^1/_2$ cup sugar (125 ml) }	Whip 2-3 minutes until thick and yellow.
2 tsp peach liqueur (10 ml)	Add, mixing well.
$^1/_3$ cup flour (75 ml)	Fold in gently to above mixture.
6 egg whites	Beat in clean bowl until soft peaks form.
2 tbsp sugar (30 ml)	Add to egg whites and beat until stiff.
	Gently fold egg whites into above yolk-flour mixture until whites disappear. Pour evenly into pan and bake approx. 12 minutes or until tester comes out clean. Cool on rack.

Cream

2 cups whipping cream (500 ml) $^1/_2$ cup sifting sugar (125 ml) }	Whip until stiff.
$^1/_3$ cup peach liqueur or schnapps (75 ml) $^1/_2$ tsp grated orange rind (2 ml) }	Fold into cream/sugar mixture.
1 tsp gelatin (5 ml)	Dissolve according to package and add when cool; set aside.
8 oz. canned or fresh peaches (250 ml)	Slice thinly and set aside.

Assembly

Brush some raspberry jam over sponge layer. Cut evenly into three sections. Place one layer on serving dish and put some whipped cream on top. Place some peach slices on top. Repeat for the other two layers. Ice the entire cake with remaining cream. Decorate with peaches.

Mixed Fruit Pound Cake

Preheat oven to 350°F (180°C).
9 x 5 x 3" loaf pan, well buttered and floured (23 x 12 x 7 cm)

1 cup butter (250 ml)
1 cup sugar (250 ml) } Whip until creamy and fluffy.

grated rind of one lemon
1 1/2 tbsp lemon juice (22 ml)
2 tsp vanilla (10 ml) } Add to above, beating until blended.

5 eggs   Add one at a time, beating each well.

2 scant cups of flour (500 ml)
1 cup mixed candied fruit (250 ml) } Add and mix on low speed just until combined. Do not overbeat. Pour into pan. Bake approx. 50-55 minutes or until tester comes out clean. Cool on rack. Sprinkle with icing sugar.

Great morning bread or afternoon tea cake.

ESTHER KRAVICE AND MARY SOMERTON

Nine years ago two sisters, both crazy about desserts, decided to bake out of their home, helping to fill the enormous demand by Toronto restaurants for good pastries. The response to the extraordinary desserts which Esther and Mary produced was phenomenal and soon they opened a shop on Dupont Street. Their entire business is to wholesalers and has built tremendously, all through word-of-mouth.

Both sisters believe that the reasons for their continued success are service, quality, consistency and innovation. They are always creating new desserts and have 40 varieties to date, including 25 flavours of cheesecake.

Their philosophy is to use only natural ingredients to obtain the best flavour possible. Once their requirement is met, appearance is the next important step.

Cheesecakes and chocolate desserts seem to be the favourites of their clientèle, who are spread all over the city. Appearing in *The Dessert Scene* will certainly bring them to the awareness of both bakers and tasters. Enjoy their famous Kahlua Truffle Cake and Raspberry Bombe.

Hazelnut Dacquoise

Preheat oven to 300°F (150°C).
3 large cookie pans lined with buttered parchment paper. Draw three
 8" circles onto paper.

10 egg whites	Beat until half their volume.
2 tbsp sugar (30 ml)	Add, beating until stiff.
1 cup ground toasted hazelnuts (250 ml) 1 cup sugar (250 ml)	Mix together in bowl.
2 cups icing sugar (500 ml) 1 tbsp cornstarch (15 ml)	Sift into nut mixture. Fold carefully into egg whites.

Using pastry bag or spoon, pipe in circles with egg white mixture onto
cookie sheet. Pipe long cylinder shapes with remaining mixture beside
the circles. Bake for one hour and fifteen minutes. If meringues begin to
brown too quickly, rearrange pan locations or lower heat. Cool on rack.
Invert carefully.

Buttercream

$^3/_4$ cup sugar (175 ml) $^1/_2$ cup corn syrup (125 ml)	Stir over medium heat until mixture boils. Remove from heat.
4 large egg yolks	In clean bowl whip until thick and pale. Beat in sugar mixture until cool, approx. 5 minutes.
1 $^3/_4$ cup butter (425 ml)	Beat into above, piece by piece.
$^1/_4$ cup nut liqueur (50 ml)	Mix into above. Refrigerate until consistency is suitable for icing.

Assembly

Ice each meringue layer with half of the buttercream and then use the
remainder for the tops and sides. Crush piped cylinder pieces of
meringue and decorate cake on top and sides with these pieces.

Kahlua Truffle Cake

Preheat oven to 350°F (180°C).
9" springform lined with buttered parchment paper (22 cm).

Chocolate Sponge

3 egg yolks } 1/4 cup sugar (50 ml) }	Beat about two minutes, until light in colour.
1 tsp vanilla(5 ml)	Add and blend.
1 1/2 tbsp cocoa (22 ml) } 1 tbsp flour (15 ml) }	Fold into above mixture. Combine gently.
3 egg whites	Whip until soft peaks form.
1/4 cup sugar (50 ml)	Beat in until stiff, folding quickly into above. Pour into pan. Bake approx. 20 minutes or until tester comes out clean. Cool on rack.

Dessert Syrup

1/4 cup sugar (50 ml) } 1/4 cup water (50 ml) }	Boil. Set aside to cool.

Truffle

8 oz. semisweet chocolate (250 g)	Melt and set aside.
3/4 cup butter (175 ml) } 1/2 cup icing sugar (125 ml) }	Beat until soft and creamy.
1/4 cup cocoa (50 ml) } 1/4 cup Kahlua (50 ml) }	Combine with butter mixture. Add melted chocolate and beat slowly until well mixed.
1 egg	Add and mix.
1 cup whipping cream, room temperature (250 ml)	Add slowly and blend until smooth. Set aside.

Ganache

6 oz. semisweet chocolate(170g)	Melt.
1/2 cup whipping cream (125 ml)	Add slowly to above and mix. If the ganache hardens before use, reheat slightly until it is of spreading consistency.

Assembly

Brush sponge layer with dessert syrup. Pour truffle mixture on top and level. Refrigerate approx. 1 hour. When set, pour ganache over top. Sprinkle with toasted sliced almonds.

Raspberry Bombe

Preheat oven to 350°F (180°C). 10-12" (25 - 30 cm) pan lined with buttered, floured parchment paper.

White Sponge

6 egg yolks } 1/2 cup sugar (125 ml) }	Beat until light in colour, approx. 2 minutes.
2 tsp vanilla (10 ml)	Add and blend.
1/3 cup flour (75 ml)	Fold in gently until blended. Do not overmix.
6 egg whites	Beat until soft peaks form.
1/4 cup sugar (50 ml)	Beat in sugar until stiff. Fold quickly into above mixture. Pour into pan and bake approx. 20-25 minutes, or until tester comes out clean. Cool on rack.

Dessert Syrup

1/4 cup sugar (50 ml) } 1/4 cup water (50 ml) }	Boil. Set aside to cool. Add a little liqueur of choice to taste.

Raspberry Mousse

3/4 cup raspberry purée (175 ml) } 6 tbsp icing sugar (90 ml) }	Mix until sugar dissolves.
1 tbsp gelatin (15 ml)	Dissolve according to package. When melted, add to purée mix.
1 1/2 cups whipping cream (375 ml)	Whip until soft peaks form. Fold into raspberry mixture. Set aside.

Ganache

6 oz semisweet chocolate (170 g)	Melt and cool slightly.
1/3 cup whipping cream (75 ml)	Slowly add to chocolate and mix well. Set aside.
2 tbsp fruit or jelly glaze (30 ml)	Melt and save for bombe.

Assembly

Carefully slice sponge lengthwise into two layers. Gently lift one layer with spatulas and place into 8 cup (2 l) kitchen bowl . Brush with some dessert syrup. Pour mousse on top. Trim other sponge layer to fit mousse still in bowl. Carefully lift and place over mousse in bowl. Brush with some dessert syrup. Refrigerate for 2-4 hours. Unmold by dipping sides of bowl into sink of hot water for five seconds then invert onto a serving plate. Glaze with jelly and pour ganache over bombe until smooth. Sprinkle with chopped pistachios (optional).

Bear Essentials

NANCY GANGBAR

Four years ago Nancy made truffles in her home for friends and acquaintances. As a lark, one day she created an arrangement of chocolate bears on skis for a ski lover. It was so popular that personalized requests came pouring in and since that time Nancy has been designing chocolate tennis racquets, houses, mountains, wine bottles and anything else her customers can imagine.

A love of chocolate and artistry encouraged her to open Bear Essentials, located in the prestigious Forest Hill area of Toronto. Her products range through every type of truffle imaginable, from·cookies and chocolates to her mainstay, personalized chocolate baskets.

Nancy has never advertised but word-of-mouth has spread her business like wildfire. She believes her success is due to creativity plus the use of the finest and freshest ingredients available. Her chocolates are made fresh each week.

The high-point in Nancy's career so far came when a Montreal TV show commissioned her to design a chocolate weekend in Toronto as a prize. In a luxurious hotel room, Nancy made sure that *everything* was chocolate, including the telephone and the lights.

Enjoy the champagne, Grand Marnier and white chocolate truffles that Nancy has shared with us.

White Chocolate
Grand Marnier Truffle

Makes two dozen.

1/3 cup whipping cream (75 ml)	Scald in saucepan. Remove from heat and cool to room temperature.
8 oz. white chocolate (250 g)	Break into smaller pieces and melt.
2 tbsp soft butter (30 ml)	Beat into chocolate until smooth.
	Beat whipping cream into chocolate mixture vigorously until light and fluffy.
1/8 cup Grand Marnier (25 ml)	Beat into above until mixed. Chill for 1-2 hours until firm.
8 oz. white chocolate (250 g)	Melt in bowl. Roll truffle mixture into balls and dip in melted chocolate. Place on waxed paper and chill until firm.

Champagne Truffle

Makes two dozen.

8 oz. milk chocolate (250 g)	Break into small pieces and melt.
1/2 cup soft butter (125 ml)	Beat into chocolate vigorously.
1/4 cup champagne (50 ml)	Beat into above until well mixed. Chill 1-2 hours until firm.
1 cup icing sugar (250 ml)	Roll truffle mixture into balls and roll in sugar. Refrigerate.

Nut Truffle

Makes two dozen.

4 oz. milk chocolate (125 g) 4 oz. semisweet chocolate (125 g)	Break into smaller pieces and melt.
$1/2$ cup soft butter (125 ml)	Beat into melted chocolate vigorously until light and fluffy.
$1/4$ cup finely chopped toasted almonds (50 ml)	Combine with above. Refrigerate 1-2 hours until hard enough to roll.
1 cup coarsely chopped toasted almonds (250 ml)	Roll truffle mixture into balls and then roll in almonds. Store in cool place.

CAROLE OGUS

No name in Toronto is more synonymous with exciting high-quality cheesecakes than Carole.

It was Carole's wonderful husband who taught her to cook. Soon she began experimenting with baking, creating such fabulous desserts that friends started asking her to bake for social functions.

Fifteen years ago nothing in terms of natural and "homey" desserts existed in Toronto. Carole decided to change all that. She was working seven days a week as a teacher but soon took up baking and opened her first store on Eglinton Street West. Her début cheesecake–toasted almond–garnered such rave responses in restaurants that requests for other flavours began to pour in. Soon she had 80 varieties of cheesecake and 15 other specialty cakes for sale. Carole now has franchises and outlets throughout Ontario.

Continued success has come through quality control. Carole emphasizes that recipes have never altered and her prices remain reasonable for the quality. She still uses all natural ingredients.

Carole's desserts are unusual in that they can be frozen for up to nine months without losing either taste or texture. Ultimately she hopes to expand into the United States and Europe and have her family enter the business.

Apple Cinnamon Cheesecake

Preheat oven to 325°F (160°C).
9" (22 cm) springform pan.

Crust

2 cups graham wafer crumbs (500 ml)
1/2 cup sugar (125 ml)
1/2 tsp cinnamon (2 ml)
1/2 cup melted butter (125 ml)

Mix in bowl. Put into bottom and sides of pan. Refrigerate while preparing the filling.

Filling

1 1/2 lb. cream cheese (375 g)

Beat until smooth.

1 cup sugar (250 ml)
4 eggs
1 tsp vanilla (5 ml)
1 tsp lemon juice (5 ml)

Add, beating well until smooth. Scrape the sides.

1 cup diced apple (250 ml)

Peel, core and dice in small bowl.

1 tbsp flour (15 ml)
1 tbsp cinnamon (15 ml)

Mix into apples to coat.

Fold apple mixture into cheesecake batter. Add more cinnamon to taste. Pour into pan. Bake 55-60 minutes or until centre is slightly loose. Cool on rack for 20 minutes. Leave oven on. Meanwhile, make topping.

Topping

2 cups sour cream (500 ml)
1/4 cup sugar (50 ml)
1 tsp vanilla (5 ml)

Mix until well blended. Pour over cake and put back into oven for 15 minutes.

Cool on rack and then refrigerate for 3-4 hours.

The combination of apples, cinnamon and cheese is unbelievable!

Sour Cream Chocolate Brownies

Preheat oven to 325°F (160°C).
8 x 8" square buttered and floured pan (20 x 20 cm).

8 oz. semisweet chocolate (250 g)	Melt and set aside to cool slightly.
2 eggs	Add to above mixing well.
4 oz. butter (125 ml)	Melt in small bowl.
3/4 cups sugar (175 ml)	Add to butter, mix and then add to chocolate mixture.
1/3 cup sour cream (75 ml) 2 tsp vanilla (10 ml)	Add to above, mixing well.
3/4 cup flour (175 ml) 1 tsp baking powder (15 ml)	Add, stirring just until blended.
optional - 1/2 cup chocolate chips (125 g)	Blend quickly into above.
	Pour into pan and bake approximately 25-30 minutes or until centre is just a little soft. Cool on rack before cutting.

The moistest brownies ever!

Georgian Cake

Preheat oven to 325°F (160°C).
Butter and flour large springform (10-12") (25-30 cm).

Cake

16 oz chopped pitted dates (500 g) 2 cups water (500 ml)	Simmer over heat 10-15 minutes, stirring until mixture resembles purée. Cool.
1 $^1/_2$ tsp baking soda (7 ml)	Stir into above.
$^1/_4$ lb butter (125 ml)	In clean bowl, cream.
1 $^1/_2$ cups sugar (375 ml) 2 eggs	Beat into butter and add to dates.
2 $^1/_2$ cups flour (625 ml) 2 tsp baking powder (10 ml)	Alternate folding into egg mixture with dates until blended. Pour into pan. Bake 1 $^1/_4$ to 1 $^1/_2$ hours or until tester comes out clean. Set on rack while making topping. Increase oven heat to broil.

Topping

$^1/_2$ cup + 2 tbsps. butter (145 ml) 6 tbsp 10% cream (90 ml) $^1/_2$ cup brown sugar (125 ml)	Combine in saucepan over medium heat. Boil 3 minutes, stirring occasionally. Remove from heat.
1 cup shredded unsweetened coconut (250 ml)	Stir into above and spread over warm cake.
	Place under broiler one minute or until coconut turns light brown. Cool before removing sides of pan.

An incredibly moist cake that keeps fresh for days!

Dessert Peddler

MARY ANN MORAN

Believe it or not, only minutes away from greater Metropolitan Toronto there's a town that has the ambiance and nostalgic feel of an old-fashioned rural village. The place is Unionville and here you can find good homey desserts just like the ones Grandmother used to make.

Mary Ann Moran, like many other successful women in the food trade, began working out of her home. Eight years ago she baked for a restaurant in Unionville and eventually was forced to open a storefront herself, which she did, right on Main Street. The store was an instant success. Many of her customers travel over 30 miles to buy Mary Ann's treats because there are few places left that sell good old-fashioned desserts like butter tarts, Nanaimo bars, carrot cake, date squares, and traditional chocolate cake.

Mary Ann bakes everything from scratch and uses the finest ingredients for all her desserts. Tasting is believing as you will discover when you try her "homey" goodness.

Rich Chocolate Cheesecake

Preheat oven to 250°F (120°C).
9" springform (22 cm).

Crust

2 cups graham crumbs (500 ml)
1 1/2 tbsp cocoa (22 ml)
3 tbsp melted butter (45 ml)

Combine and press along sides and bottoms of pan. Bake 15 minutes and cool.

Increase oven heat to 350°F (180°C).

Cake

24 oz. cream cheese (750 grams)

Whip well.

1 cup sugar (250 ml)

Add and beat, scraping sides.

3 tbsp flour (45 ml)
3 eggs
2 tbsp sour cream (30 ml)
2 tsp vanilla (10 ml)
2 tbsp cocoa (30 ml)

Add to above beating well. Scrape sides.

6 oz. melted semisweet chocolate (170 g)

Add to above, beating quickly until well combined.

Pour into crust and bake approx. 40-45 minutes until centre is still a little loose. Cool and refrigerate. Garnish with shaved chocolate and whipped cream if desired.

Fudge-like quality of cheesecake.

Old Fashioned Carrot Cake

Preheat oven to 350°F (180°C).
2 round 9" buttered and floured pans (22 cm).

Cake

4 eggs	Beat in large bowl.
1 1/2 cups sugar (375 ml)	Beat in sugar until blended.
1 1/2 cups oil (375 ml)	Add and beat slowly until mixed.
* 1 cup cake flour (250 ml) * 1 cup all-purpose flour (250 ml) 1 tsp baking soda (5 ml) 2 tsp baking powder (10 ml) 2 tsp cinnamon (10 ml)	Sift and add into above with wooden spoon. Do not overmix.
1 1/2 cup walnuts (375 ml) 1 cup raisins (250 ml) 3 cups grated carrots (750 ml)	Fold into above just until blended.

Note: Two types of flour give a lighter texture.

Pour into pans and bake 35-40 minutes or until tester comes out clean.
Cool on rack and invert. Ice.

Old Fashioned Butter Cream Cheese Icing

2 egg whites	Whip until stiff.
1 1/4 cups icing sugar (300 ml)	Add and combine well.
5 oz. soft butter (150 ml)	Add and beat well.
4 oz. soft vegetable shortening (125 ml)	Add and beat well.
1/2 tsp vanilla (2 ml) 4 oz. soft cream cheese (125 g)	Add and beat until lumps disappear.

Layer cakes and ice in between, sides and top.
Decorate with toasted coconut or toasted nuts.

Old Fashioned Chocolate Chip Cookies

Preheat oven to 350°F (180°C).
Grease two cookie sheets.

1 cup butter (250 ml) $^1/2$ cups white sugar (125 ml) $^3/4$ cup brown sugar (175 ml) }	Beat until creamy.
1 tsp vanilla (5 ml) 2 eggs }	Add to above mixing well.
2 $^1/4$ cup flour (550 ml) 1 tsp baking soda (5 ml) }	Add to above, mixing just until blended.
2 cups chocolate chips (500 g)	Fold into above. Better if dough is chilled for 30 minutes.

Drop by spoonfuls on cookie sheets and bake for approx. 10-12 minutes or until tester comes out clean and bottoms begins to brown.

Rhubarb Custard Tart

Preheat oven to 375°F (190°C).
8" springform (20 cm).

Crust

1 1/2 cups flour (375 ml)
1/3 cup icing sugar (75 ml) } Combine.

6 oz. butter (175 ml) — Cut in until well combined. Processor can be used.

Put into bottom and sides of pan. Prebake until light brown (15-20 minutes). Meanwhile, prepare topping and filling. Cool on rack.

Topping

1 cup chopped nuts (250 ml)
1/2 cup flour (125 ml)
1/3 cup brown sugar (75 ml)
1/3 cup white sugar (75 ml)
1 tbsp cinnamon (15 ml) } Combine in bowl.

1/2 cup soft butter (125 ml) — Add butter until mixture is crumbly. Set aside.

Pie

5 cups sliced rhubarb
(1 L. 250 ml) frozen or fresh
(must be defrosted) — Place in crust.

1/4 cup melted butter (50 ml)
3 tbsp flour(45 ml) } Mix in small bowl.

1 cup sugar (250 ml)
2 eggs } Add to above butter-flour and mix well. Pour over rhubarb into crust. Sprinkle topping over rhubarb.

Bake for 35-45 minutes or until rhubarb is tender. If topping begins to brown too quickly, cover with foil. Cool on rack.

Harvest Pie

Preheat oven to 375°F (190°C).
9" springform (22 cm).

Crust

1 1/2 cups flour (375 ml)
1/3 cup sifting sugar (75 ml) } Combine.

6 oz. butter (175 ml) — Cut in butter until combined. Put into bottom and sides of pan. Prebake (15-20 minutes) until golden brown. Cool on rack. Make topping.

Topping

1/2 cup flour (125 ml)
1 tbsp cinnamon (15 ml)
2/3 cup sugar (150 ml)
1 cup chopped pecans (250 ml) } Combine in bowl.

1/2 cup butter (125 ml) — Add butter until crumbly. Set aside.

Pie

2 cups sliced apples (500 ml)
1 cup sliced pears (250 ml)
1 cup mandarin oranges (250 ml)
1 cup raisins (250 ml)
3/4 cup sugar (175 ml)
1/4 cup flour (50 ml)
1 tsp cinnamon (5 ml)
1/4 tsp nutmeg (1 ml) } Toss together in bowl until dry ingredients coat the fruit. Pour into crust. Sprinkle on topping. Bake approximately 45 minutes or until fruit is tender.

There has never been a pie created like this!

DUFFLET ROSENBERG

Dufflet is *not* a type of fancy French pastry. It is the unusual nickname, chosen at a young age, by one of Toronto's most dynamic and successful female bakers. But no matter the origin of the name, Dufflet is synonymous with decadent and beautiful desserts.

Twelve years ago Dufflet began, like many food entrepreneurs, by baking out of her home. She sold desserts to the Cow Café and was offered a position there as the baker. Later she decided to travel to New York and then to France to study. In 1980 she opened her famous retail spot on Queen Street and in 1985 set up facilities in a factory for the wholesale trade, the mainstay of her business.

Dufflet has a variety of desserts, between 40 and 50, her menu rotating monthly. Her two premier attractions have always been the white chocolate mousse and almond meringue cakes, although now the trend seems to be heading towards her fruit desserts.

Dufflet frequently travels to other cities for ideas and she finds that Toronto's standards are among the best.

Her tip to bakers is to make what *you* like, not what seems to be trendy. A combination of "homey" and attractive desserts are the results people are looking for today.

It is very common to find her name mentioned regularly in food sections of magazines and newspapers. This type of recognition no longer fazes Dufflet, who works continuously to assure her long-term success. As well as being both a business-woman and baker, when given the opportunity, she also loves to teach.

Enjoy her natural and "homey" delicacies!

Swiss Chocolate Layered Mousse Cake

Preheat oven to 400°F (200°C).
2 9" buttered & floured cake pans lined with parchment paper (22 cm).

Cake

8 oz. soft butter (250 ml)	Cream with mixer until fluffy.
1 $^1/_2$ cups sugar (375 ml)	Add and continue creaming.
2 egg whites	Add to above and continue to cream, until very light.
2 cups sifted cake flour (500 ml) 2 $^1/_2$ tsp baking powder (12 ml) $^1/_4$ tsp salt (1 ml)	Sift together in clean bowl.
1 cup milk (250 ml) 1 tsp vanilla (5 ml)	Add milk, vanilla and dry ingredients alternatively to above butter mixture. End with flour. Mix until combined.
3 egg whites	Whip in clean bowl until soft peaks form.
1 tsp sugar (5 ml)	Add and whip until stiff.
	Fold carefully into above flour and butter mixture just until whites are incorportaed. Divide into pans, bake approximately 25-30 minutes until tester comes out dry and cake pulls away from side of pan. Remove from oven and cool on rack.

Syrup

$^1/_2$ cup water (125 ml) $^1/_4$ cup sugar (50 ml)	Bring to boil. Cool and add a little liquor of choice.

$\triangleright$

Sweet Sue Pastries

Chocolate Torte (Chocolate dipped strawberries)

Bear Essentials

White Grand Marnier Truffles
Nut Truffles
Champagne Truffles

Swiss Chocolate Layered Mousse Cake
(continued)

Mousse

1 lb semisweet Swiss chocolate (500 g) $^2/_3$ lbs. butter (330 ml) }	Melt together and cool to room temperature.
8 egg yolks	Blend into above mixture.
2 tsp gelatin (10 ml)	Dissolve according to package and add to above.
8 egg whites	Whip in clean dry bowl until soft peaks form.
$^1/_2$ cup sugar (125 ml)	Add to whites and beat until stiff. Fold into chocolate mixture carefully.
1 cup whipping cream (250 ml)	Whip until stiff. Fold into above.

Assembly

Slice cool cakes lengthwise into two halves. Place one half into 9" springform (22 cm). Brush with dessert syrup. Top with one cup mousse (250 ml). Repeat. Before icing top and sides, refrigerate until mousse has reset. Unmold cake and ice top and sides with remaining mousse. Decorate all over, or just top with chocolate curls. (Grate a slab of chocolate with a vegetable peeler.)

$\lhd$

Four Seasons Hotel
(plaited desserts)

Raspberry Mousse on a cream cheese gratin
Peach yogurt timbales with strawberry cream

Strawberry Rhubarb Linzer Pie

Preheat oven to 400°F (200°C).
Butter 10" springform (25 cm).

Crust

1 cup chilled butter (250 ml)	Cut into small pieces.
1 cup sugar (250 ml)	Add to butter in food processor, Blend until creamy.
2 cups flour (500 ml) 9 oz. ground almonds (260 ml) $^1/_2$ tsp cinnamon (2 ml) Pinch of clove	Add to above mixture until it gets crumbly.
2 egg yolks	Combine with above until mixture holds together. Use hands if necessary. Refrigerate $1^1/_2$ hour. Prepare the filling.

Filling

1 oz. butter (30 ml) $^1/_4$ cup sugar (50 ml)	Melt in large pot.
1 $^1/_4$ lbs rhubarb cut into small pieces (625 ml) (If frozen, defrost)	Stir into above and cook over medium heat until fork tender. Strain off juice, reserve. Keep rhubarb on stove at low heat.
1 tbsp corn starch (15 ml)	Add to rhubarb juice and mix.
$^1/_4$ cup sugar (50 ml)	Add to rhubarb juice and mix. Stir this into rhubarb and cook until thickened.
$^1/_2$ lb. strawberries (250 ml) 1 orange rind, grated	Stir into above and remove from heat. Cool.

Assembly

Remove dough from refrigerator and when soft enough take two-thirds and press into bottom and sides of pan with fingers. Pour filling into crust. Crumble remaining dough on top of filling. Bake 15 minutes and lower oven temp. to 325°F (160°C) for another 20 minutes, or until crust is golden brown. Cool completely before serving.

This nutty crust with strawberries and rhubarb is sensational!

Fenton's

WERNER BASSEN

Fenton's has always been associated with class, sophistication and haute cuisine, and rightfully so. This chic restaurant in the heart of downtown Toronto, with its three separate dining experiences as well as a wonderful retail gourmet shop, has tripled in size over the past nine years.

Werner Bassen, Fenton's original pastry chef, began his career at the age of 14 as a cook in Germany. He worked in Europe for a time before he received an offer to cook at a hotel in Niagara-on-the-Lake. In 1976 he was given the opportunity to open Fenton's as executive chef.

Werner entered into the pastry end of the business and now loves both cooking and creating desserts. He jumps from the bakery to the prep kitchen to the line—and expresses his many talents to the appreciation of all customers. He believes that Fenton's clientele are people who love rich desserts and are willing to pay for top quality.

In the spring of 1986 Werner appeared in *Toronto Life Epicure*, featuring his white and dark chocolate paté which has been included in the book. His choices are incredibly simple and elegant.

White and Dark Chocolate Mousse Paté

Preheat oven to 325°F (160°C).
8-9" buttered springform pan lined with buttered parchment paper
    (20-22 cm).

Dark Chocolate

8 oz. semisweet chocolate (250 g)	Melt. Cool slightly. Set aside.
6 egg yolks	Beat until light in colour.
$^1/_2$ cups sugar (125 ml)	Add to yolks, mixing well.
1 tsp vanilla (5 ml)	Combine with yolks and then beat mixture lightly into chocolate, until blended.
6 egg whites	Beat until stiff. Gently fold into above.

Pour into a pan. Bake 20-25 minutes or until centre only is a bit loose.
Turn off heat and let rest in oven 5 more minutes. Cool on rack in pan.

White Chocolate (Unbaked)

8 oz. white chocolate (250 g)	Melt. Set aside.
6 egg yolks	Beat until light in colour. Pour chocolate in eggs and mix with spoon until blended.
1 package gelatin	Dissolve according to package and then mix into above. Cool slightly.
2 cups whipping cream (500 ml)	Whip until stiff. Fold quickly into above. Pour over cooled dark chocolate and refrigerate at least 2 hours. Meanwhile prepare sauces (optional).

White and Dark Chocolate Mousse Paté (continued)

Note: This dessert is wonderful even without sauces, or with just one sauce. Both sauces make it complete.

Raspberry Sauce

2 cups fresh or frozen raspberries (500 ml)
3 tbsp icing sugar (45 ml)
1 tbsp lemon juice (15 ml)

Purée. Set aside.

Sabayon

3 egg yolks
$1/2$ cup sugar (125 ml)
$1/4$ cup rum (50 ml)

In double boiler, over simmering heat, beat mixture briskly. Do not let bowl touch water. When smooth like custard, remove from heat and whisk for 3-4 more minutes. Cool.

1 cup whipping cream (250 ml)

Whip until stiff, and fold into above.

Assembly

Remove sides of pan and cut slices to be served with sauce(s).

This is an award winning dessert of Fenton's!

Fenton's Cointreau
Mousse Gâteau

Preheat oven to 325° (160°)
Buttered and floured 8" springform (20cm)

8 oz. chocolate (250 g)	Melt in microwave or double boiler, cool slightly.
6 egg yolks 1/2 cup sugar (125 ml) }	Beat until pale and thick.
1/4 cup Cointreau or orange liqueur (50 ml) 1 tsp vanilla (5 ml) 1 finely grated orange rind }	Add to above, beat lightly until blended. Set aside.
6 egg whites	Beat until stiff and gently fold into above until all whites disappear.

Assembly

Pour 2/3 of mixture into pan. Set remaining 1/3 aside and chill. Bake for approx. 20 minutes or until cake looks done and only centre is a little loose. Turn off heat and let cake rest in oven for an extra five minutes. Slightly cool on rack. Fill cake with remaining cold mousse.
Refrigerate until set. Garnish with icing sugar and chocolate shavings.

Unusual combination of baked and unbaked mousse!

Espresso and Sambucca Brûlée

Preheat oven to 350°F (180°C).

6 – 7 individual serving custard cups

1 1/2 cups whipping cream (375 ml)
1/2 cup prepared espresso or strong
coffee (125 ml)
1/4 cup Sambucca
or any licorice liqueur (50 ml)
3 tbsp sugar (45 ml)
4 egg yolks
2 whole eggs

Combine all ingredients and pour into cups.

Place cups in larger pan filled with hot water. (Bain-marie)

Bake approx. 20 minutes or until centre is set. Increase heat to broil.

Brown sugar

Sprinkle a little on each cup, return to oven just until top bubbles. Remove and repeat. Cool on rack.

Chill in refrigerator.

Coffee and licorice create an explosion of flavours!

Cream Cups on a Strawberry Purée

6 – 8 individual molds with holes in the bottom for drainage, or make your own by puncturing holes in aluminum muffin or custard cups.

1 lb. cream cheese (500 g)
3 tbsp sugar (45 ml) } Beat until smooth.

1 cup whipping cream (250 ml) Whip until stiff peaks form. Fold into above mixture.

3 egg whites In clean bowl, beat until stiff and fold into above mixture.

Line molds with pieces of cheesecloth.* Pour filling into lined molds, fold cheesecloth over top, place on tray and then refrigerate for approx. 6 hours, so excess liquid can drain. Carefully turn out, and then remove cheesecloth. Serve with strawberry purée.

Purée

2 cups fresh or frozen
strawberries (500 ml)
3 tbsp icing sugar (45 ml)
1 tbsp lemon juice (15 ml) } Purée and serve with cream cups.

* Cheesecloth can be bought in specialty cookstores, or can be substituted with J-cloths or sterile gauze pads. All will work.

"Snow Eggs" – Oeufs à la Neige

4 individual small glass bowls   4 servings

2 cups milk (500 ml)	Pour into large saucepan over medium heat.
3 egg whites	In clean bowl, beat until stiff.
6 tbsp sugar (90 ml)	Add gradually to egg whites until sugar dissolves.

With a large serving spoon, form 4 egg-shaped meringues and place into almost boiling milk. Poach for approx. 1-2 minutes, turn onto the other side and poach for another minute. Remove snow eggs with slotted spoon and serve cold in a bowl filled with crème anglaise. Sprinkle with chopped pistachios.

Crème anglaise

4 egg yolks $^1/_2$ cup sugar (125 ml) }	Beat until thick.
2 cups 10 or 18% cream (500 ml)	Heat in saucepan almost to boiling. Put a little into the yolk mixture and pour back into remaining cream. Beat lightly on low heat until thick enough to coat a spoon. Do not let mixture boil. Remove from heat.
1 tsp vanilla (5 ml)	Add, mix and cool.

Four Seasons Hotel

WOLFGANG von WIESER

No other hotel chain is so well known in North America as the Four Seasons. Synonymous with elegance and sophistication, the Toronto hotel, situated in the most expensive and fashionable area of town, is one of the best in North America.

Their well-known dining-room, Truffles, features Austrian chef Wolfgang von Wieser. Wolfgang apprenticed in Switzerland and then worked at numerous five-star hotels, one of which was The Kuhn in St. Moritz. From France he went to London and then came to Canada about one and a half years ago. His first job at the Four Seasons was executive sous chef. Because he loves working with his hands and being as creative as possible, five months ago he was made pastry chef.

Wolfgang's pet peeve in pastry is that most Toronto chefs don't pay attention to the seasons. He believes that the fresher the fruit and other ingredients the better, as opposed to using fruit out-of-season which tends to be very costly and usually not as ripe or fresh.

Wolfgang won a silver medal at the Toronto Food and Wine Show for four different plaited desserts. He features some of these specialties in *The Dessert Scene.*

In the future, Wolfgang sees himself returning to Europe because he misses the culture. He also hopes to pursue a career in writing food books and calendars.

Raspberry Mousse on an Orange Cream Cheese Gratin

2 cup mold (500 ml)   4 servings (*Recipe can be doubled*)

Mousse

$^1/_4$ cup sugar (50 ml)
$^3/_4$ cup raspberry purée (175 ml)   } Purée until smooth.

$^1/_2$ package gelatin   Melt according to package then add to above purée.
Place in refrigerator to thicken.

1 cup whipping cream (250 ml)   Whip until stiff, fold into gelled mixture. Pour into mold. Set in refrigerator 2–2$^1/_2$ hours.

Gratin

4 tbsp cream cheese (60 g)
2 egg yolks
2 tsp sugar (10 ml)   } Mix in food processor until blended. Set aside.

1 grated rind of orange
1 tbsp sugar (15 ml)   } Chop in food processor and remove. Place in cup and cover with hot water for 2 minutes. Strain. Add to cream cheese mixture. Pour onto ovenproof serving dish and place under broiler until light brown. Cool.

Assembly

Turn out mousse by dipping mold in hot water for approx.
5 seconds. Invert onto gratin dish. Sprinkle with chopped pistachios.

Peach Yogurt Terrine
with Strawberry Cream

2 cup mold or 4 individual molds (500 ml)   Serves 4.
(Recipe can be doubled)

3 1/2 oz. peach yogurt (100 ml)
3/4 cup peach purée
(canned or fresh) (175 ml)
1/3 cup sugar (75 ml) } Blend well in bowl.

1/2 package gelatin Dissolve according to package then add to above mixture.

1/2 cup whipping cream (125 ml) Whip until stiff and fold into above. Pour into mold and refrigerate for two hours. Prepare sauce.

Strawberry Cream

1/2 cup strawberry purée (125 ml)
2 tbsp sour cream (30 ml)
2 tbsp icing sugar (30 ml) } Combine and blend well.

Place mold(s) into pan of hot water for approx. 5 seconds. Carefully invert onto serving plate(s) and serve with strawberry cream. Decorate with fresh fruit.

Apricot Suzettes
with Cinnamon Vanilla

4-5 servings

3 $^{1}/_{2}$ oz. apricots (100 ml)	Soak in hot water for 1 hour.
1 tbsp apricot brandy (15 ml) 1 tsp sugar (5 ml)	Add to apricots and cook until soft (15-20 minutes). Drain well and dice finely.
1 bag won ton sheets Handful of mint leaves	Separate one sheet carefully and place on floured board. Brush with water. Place one mint leaf on top. Cover with another sheet. Use rolling pin to flatten until sheet becomes translucent.
	Place 1 tsp (5ml) of diced apricots on sheet, wet the edges. Roll separate sheet until thin and place on top of apricots. Use knife to cut out leaf shape. Repeat until diced apricots are all used. Cook apricot suzettes in simmering water for 2-3 minutes. Cool and serve with sauce. (Won ton sheets tend to be harder than other doughs.)

Cinnamon Vanilla Sauce

$^{3}/_{4}$ cup milk (175 ml) $^{1}/_{2}$ tsp vanilla (2 ml)	Simmer for 5 minutes.
2 egg yolks 1 tbsp sugar (15 ml) $^{1}/_{4}$ tsp cinnamon (1 ml)	Whisk separately until pale and pour hot milk over egg mixture. Place over double boiler, heat and stir until slightly thickened. Cool.
$^{1}/_{4}$ cup natural yogurt (50 ml)	Add when cool. Refrigerate.

Poached Pears with Cranberry and Ricotta Puffs

4 servings

Ricotta Puffs

1 cup soft ricotta cheese (250 g)
2 tbsp semolina flour (30 ml)
} Mix together in bowl.

1 tbsp soft butter (15 ml)
4 tsp sugar (20 ml)
$^1/_2$ egg
Pinch salt
} Mix in separate bowl until creamy. Add to ricotta. Let rest 20-30 minutes.

Roll into small balls. (If sticky, add a little more flour).

Place balls into pot of simmering water for 10 minutes. Turn off heat, let rest 10 more minutes. Place puffs on plate to cool slightly.

3 tbsp bread crumbs (45 ml)
1 tbsp sugar (15 ml)
1 tbsp melted butter (15 ml)
$^1/_4$ tsp cinnamon (1 ml)
} Combine until of coating consistency. Roll puffs in mixture to coat. Set aside.

Pears

2 large pears or 4 baby pears — Peel, core and cut into slices.

1 tbsp sugar (15 ml)
white wine and water
to cover pears
} Place in pot over simmering water, add pears and then poach just until pears become tender. Remove from heat and refrigerate in juice.

Poached Pears with
Cranberry and Ricotta Puffs (continued)

Cranberry

$^1/_2$ cup cranberries (125 ml)
$^1/_2$ cup sugar (125 ml)
Red wine and water to cover

Cook over simmering heat until cranberries become puréed. Add more sugar if desired.

If sauce is too sticky, add some water.

Assembly

Place some pear slices, 2 puffs and cranberry sauce on individual serving plates.

Inn on the Park
TORONTO

SITRAM SHARMA

Inn on the Park is one of the few hotels in Toronto which offer a resort-type setting. Catering for 25 years to the tastes of tourists and business people, the Inn provides an ambience that lets them feel they have escaped the big city. Swimming pools, sixteen miles of cross-country ski trails, racquet sports plus a camp for children ensure guests' complete satisfaction.

Another outstanding feature of the Inn on the Park is pastry chef Sitram Sharma. Sitram left Guyana in 1970 in order to study English. In 1981 he came to Canada and worked at the Royal York Hotel, then the Inn on the Park, followed by the Sheraton Centre and then later the CN Tower, one of his most challenging positions because there were 1500 desserts required weekly.

Sitram decided that he enjoyed his work most at the Inn on the Park and returned there as executive pastry chef, supervising 14 people. Job satisfaction is everything to him and he has the freedom at the Inn on the Park to create whatever desserts he chooses. You'll see by this selection that he makes excellent use of this opportunity.

Sitram loves Toronto and believes that it is the ideal place to live because competition is intense, allowing only the best to succeed.

He has found lately that people are demanding more mousse-type desserts because they appear lighter than most and has met this need by making numerous varieties. His love and expertise lie in sugar and chocolate work and he has won gold medals at food and wine shows for his spectacular creations.

Sitram's future plans are to have his own café. One will understand why, after trying his desserts.

▷

Fenton's

White and Dark Chocolate Mousse Pâté
with sabayon and raspberry sauce

Orange Cheesecake

Preheat oven to 325°F (160°C).
9-10" buttered springform pan (22-25 cm)

Crust

¹/₄ cup sugar (50 ml) ⎫ grated rind of ¹/₂ small orange ⎭	Combine in processor until rind is fine chopped.
1 ¹/₂ cups vanilla wafers (375 ml)	Add, mixing until ground.
6 tbsp soft butter (90 ml)	Add until mixture holds together slightly. Put into bottom and sides of pan and chill while filling is made.

Cheesecake

6 oz. sugar (180 ml) ⎫ grated rind of ¹/₂ orange ⎭	Combine in processor until blended.
2 lbs. cream cheese (1 kg)	Add in small pieces and mix until smooth. Scrape sides.
6 eggs	Add one at a time, mixing after each.
6 oz. orange juice concentrate (180 ml)	Add then mix well.
	Pour into crust and bake 1 hour and 15 minutes or until centre is slightly loose. Cool on rack, chill and then decorate with sliced orange pieces. (Glaze with melted apple jelly if desired).
	Best served if taken out of refrigerator at least 30 minutes before serving time.

◁

L'Hôtel

Apple Torte with Almond Cream
Almond Lemon Meringue Tart

Cointreau Chocolate Decadence

10-12" springform (25-30 cm)

Crust

1 cup chocolate wafers (250 ml)	Grind until powdery.
3 tbsp melted butter (45 ml)	Add in pieces until combined. Put into bottom of pan. Refrigerate.

Filling

16 oz. semisweet chocolate (500 g)	Melt and cool slightly.
$^1/_3$ cup sugar (75 ml) 10 egg yolks }	Beat together until blended and add to chocolate.
1 package gelatin	Dissolve according to package then add to the rest.
$^1/_3$ cup Cointreau or orange liqueur (75 ml)	Add and mix well.
2 $^1/_2$ cups whipping cream (625 ml)	Whip until stiff and fold gently into above mix. Pour into crust. Freeze for a short time, until the top is hard and will hold ganache (icing).

Ganache

12 oz semisweet chocolate (375 g)	Melt and then cool slightly.
$^3/_4$ cup whipping cream (175 ml)	Slowly add to chocolate and mix until blended. If not stiff enough to glaze, refrigerate for a short time.

Assembly

When cake feels hard enough to glaze, pour ganache over top and sides and smooth. Garnish with large chocolate curls.

Cointreau Chocolate Decadence
(continued)

Note

The front cover is decorated with large sheets of shaved chocolate and a band of chocolate around the circumference of the springform.

Large Sheets of Chocolate:

Melt chocolate and pour onto marble slab. Refrigerate for a few minutes to slightly harden. When chocolate shine begins to fade, attempt to shave with large spatula. If too soft, wait a few minutes. Carefully lift and place on cake.

Band of Chocolate

Melt chocolate and pour onto strip of waxed paper, sized to fit circumference of springform. When half solid lift carefully and place strip around cake. Press lightly. When chocolate hardens, remove paper.

A heavenly dessert!

Southern Pecan Pie

Preheat oven to 350°F (180°C).
9-10" buttered flan pan (22-25 cm).

Shortbread Crust

1 1/2 cups flour (375 ml)
1/3 cup icing sugar (75 ml) } Combine in food processor.

6 oz. butter (170 ml — Add until ball forms. Put into bottom and sides of pan, and bake until slightly brown, approx. 15-20 minutes. Cool.

Pie

3 large eggs
2/3 cups sugar (150 ml) — Combine well in bowl.

1 cup corn syrup (250 ml)
2 tbsp melted butter (30 ml) } Add to above and blend well.
1 tsp vanilla (5 ml)

1 1/2 cups halved or chopped pecans (375 ml) — Fold into above. Pour into crust and bake just until centre remains a little loose, approx. 30-35 minutes.

Cool.

RICK SANDERS

Nine years ago Rick Sanders believed that Toronto desperately needed a real late-night coffee house. It turns out that he was right.

Sanders, who used to be a printer and designer, took the risk and opened Toronto's first true dessert café on Davenport Road, which was not a popular tourist street at that time. Now Just Desserts is a name that both locals and tourists know.

Even though he's never advertised, this remarkable café, which features 40 desserts on open display, has always attracted crowds. The line-ups every night of the week speak eloquently of Just Desserts' impeccable reputation.

One unusual aspect of Just Desserts is that no baking is done on the premises. Homemakers who enjoy baking produce these mouth-watering creations on a daily basis.

Although Rick has been approached on numerous occasions to expand into a more tourist-oriented area, he is not interested. He believes that the obscure location is one of the reasons why Just Desserts is what it is. He also feels that his success is due to both ambiance plus consistently high quality. It's easy to believe he's right. He features one of the best old fashioned chocolate cakes ever created. You'll agree after one mouthful.

Old Fashioned Chocolate Layer Cake

Preheat oven to 350°F (180°C).
3 9" buttered and floured layer pans (22cm).

Cake

1 1/4 cups soft butter (300 ml)
1 tbsp vanilla (15ml)
1 1/2 cups mayonnaise (375 ml)
2 2/3 cups brown sugar (650 ml)

Combine and beat until well blended.

6 eggs

Add and whip until fluffy.

3 cups flour (750 ml)
1 tbsp baking soda (15 ml)
1 1/2 cups cocoa (375 ml)
3/4 tsp salt (4 ml)

Into clean bowl, sift.

2 cups hot water (500 ml)

Add water and dry ingredients to egg mixture. Beat lightly just until lumps disappear. Do not overbeat. Pour into pans and bake. approx. 25 minutes, or until tester comes out clean. Cool 15 minutes on rack and remove from pans.

Filling

3 oz unsweetened chocolate (85 g)

Melt and set aside.

1 1/2 cups icing sugar (375 ml)
4 tbsp soft butter (60 ml)
1 egg
1 tsp vanilla (5 ml)

Add to chocolate and beat well. Refrigerate to thicken while preparing the icing.

Old Fashioned Chocolate Layer Cake
(continued)

Icing

1 $1/2$ cups icing sugar (375 ml)
$1/2$ cup warmed whipping cream (125 ml)
* 1 cup *very soft* butter (250 ml)

Whip until smooth.

1 tbsp boiling water (15 ml)

Add then beat until light and fluffy. Refrigerate while preparing cakes.

Assembly

When cakes are *completely* cool, level tops with sharp knife, so cake will not slip. Place one layer on dish and then one half filling over top. Repeat with second cake and rest of filling. Place third cake over top and frost entire cake with chilled and thickened icing. Decorate with chocolate shavings. Serve at room temperature.

* Icing will not combine unless butter is very soft.

Sour Cream Apple Pie

Preheat oven to 400°F (200°C).
Buttered and floured 9" pie pan (23cm) or 9" springform.

Pie Crust

1 1/2 cups graham wafer crumbs (375 ml)
1/2 cup melted butter (125 ml)
1/4 cup sugar (50 ml)

Combine well and press into pan. Refrigerate while preparing the filling.

Filling

1 cup sugar (250 ml)
1 1/2 cups sour cream (375 ml)
1 tsp cinnamon (5 ml)
3 tbsp flour (45 ml)
2 eggs
3/4 tsp vanilla (4 ml)

Combine and blend well.

6 medium apples

Peel, core and cut into 1" pieces and add to fluid mixture. Pour into crust. Bake for 15 minutes.

Reduce heat to 350°F (120°C).
Bake 30 minutes.
Meanwhile, make topping.

Topping

1/3 cup flour (75 ml)
3/4 tsp cinnamon (4 ml)
1/3 cup sugar (75 ml)

Combine in bowl.

3 tbsp cold butter (45 ml)

Add using fork or fingers until mixture is combined in the form of large crumbs.

After baking pie 30 minutes, raise temperature to 400°F (200°C). Sprinkle topping over pie and bake for 15 minutes until lightly browned.

King Edward Hotel

JOEL GAILLOT

With its vaulted ceilings, palm trees and marble pillars, the King Edward Hotel has been classified as one of the most elegant and luxurious hotels in downtown Toronto. Being a member of the Trusthouse Forte Executive Hotels is a distinction it shares with a very select number of other hotels and indicates that the King Edward has been designated as both distinguished and prestigious, enjoying an undisputed reputation for elegance, service and supreme excellence.

The King Eddy is fortunate enough to have a French chef, Joel Gaillot, in charge of desserts. Joel began his apprenticeship at the tender age of thirteen and before he was seventeen was employed fulltime. At nineteen he left France to work in a large hotel in Scotland and learn English. A year later he travelled to the United States and then Canada, enjoying Calgary enough to move there and work at the Four Seasons as one of their youngest pastry chefs. In 1981 he transferred to the Four Seasons in Toronto for five years before joining the King Edward a year and a half ago.

Joel finds his position challenging and exciting with lots of room to grow and expand. He focusses his expertise on sugar and chocolate. He's well known for his artistry too; he designed a chocolate statue of Beethoven which won an award. This year he's designing showpieces for the Oympics.

Joel loves Toronto because he feels that here he can be as creative as he wants. In fact, customers at the hotel's famous Café Victoria not only clamour for his creative desserts but will pay much as $12.00 for one of his unique masterpieces. His specialty in the book has been that of the world of mousses.

Frozen Maple Mousse

4 cup mold or 8 individual molds

Serves 8
(Recipe can be cut in half)

3 egg yolks
2 tbsp sugar (30 ml) } Beat until thick.

1 cup whipping cream (250 ml)   Whip until stiff. Fold into above ingredients.

3 egg whites
3 tbsp icing sugar (45 ml) } In clean bowl, beat until stiff. Fold into yolk/cream mixture.

$^1/_2$ tbsp brandy (7 ml)
$^1/_2$ tbsp maple extract (7 ml) } Fold gently into the rest.

Pour into mold and freeze for 2-4 hours. Dip mold into hot water for approx. 5 seconds and invert.

Apple Sauce Mousse with Cider Sauce

4 cup mold (1 L.) or 8 individual molds

Serves 8
(Recipe can be cut in half)

1 1/2 cups apple sauce (375 ml)
2 tsp icing sugar if apple sauce is unsweetened (10 ml) } Mix together.

1 package gelatin — Dissolve according to package and then mix into sauce.

1 1/2 cups whipping cream (375 ml) — Whip until stiff. Fold gently into gelatin mixture. Pour into mold. Chill 2-4 hours. Dip into bowl of hot water for approx. 5 seconds and invert. Serve with cider sauce.

Cider Sauce

4 egg yolks
1/2 cup sugar (125 ml) } Beat until thick.

2 cups 18% cream (500 ml) — Heat in saucepan almost to boiling. Pour a little into yolks, mix and pour back into remaining cream. Beat lightly on lowest heat until thick enough to coat a spoon. Do not let mixture boil. Remove from heat.

2 tbsp cider (30 ml) — Blend with above. If more desired, add more taste. Mix. Cool.

Pistachio Mousse

2 cup mold or 4 individual molds

Serves 4
(Recipe can be doubled)

2 egg yolks ⎫ ¹/₄ cup icing sugar (50 ml) ⎭	Beat until thick and pale yellow.
1 tsp gelatin	Dissolve according to package and then add to egg mixture.
¹/₄ cup toasted pistachio nuts (50 ml) 1 tbsp water (15 ml)	Grind to paste. Add 2 tsp nut paste to other ingredients and mix well.
1 tbsp kirsch (15 ml)	Add to mix and stir.
1 cup whipping cream (250 ml)	Whip in clean bowl until stiff. Fold into mixture.
¹/₄ cup whole toasted pistachio nuts (50 ml)	Fold into mixture.
	Pour into mold. Refrigerate for 2-4 hours. Dip into bowl of hot water for approx. 5 seconds and invert. Serve with crème anglaise.

Crème Anglaise

2 egg yolks ⎫ ¹/₄ cup sugar (50 ml) ⎭	Beat in bowl until pale yellow.
1 cup 10% or 18% cream (250 ml)	Heat in saucepan almost to boiling. Pour a little into yolks and then pour back into remaining cream. Beat lightly on low heat until thick. Do not let boil or mixture will curdle. Remove from heat.
1 tsp vanilla (5 ml)	Add and mix. Serve cold.

Mango Mousse on a Strawberry Coulis

2 cup mold or 4 individual molds

Serves 4
(Recipe can be doubled)

$^3/4$ cup mango purée (175 ml)
(1 large mango)
$^2/3$ cup sugar (150 ml)

Heat in double boiler briefly until sugar is dissolved.

$^1/2$ package gelatin

Dissolve according to package then add to purée mixture.

1 cup whipping cream (250 ml)

Whip until stiff and fold into other ingredients. Pour into mold.

Refrigerate until set, 2-3 hours.
Dip mold into pot of hot water for approx. 5 seconds.
Invert onto serving dish.

Serve with strawberry coulis on the side.

Strawberry Coulis

$^1/2$ cup puréed strawberies (125 ml)
1 tbsp icing sugar (15 ml)

Blend well.

PHILIPPE EGALON

Right in the midst of the Metro Convention Centre Complex, at the foot of the CN Tower and near the Skydome, stands L'Hôtel. A member of the CN Hotels, it is geared to business travellers and was designed with the corporate executive in mind. It is one of Toronto's only hotels to offer three different levels of treatment and accommodation. Entre Premiere is the most economical, Entre Silver is directed towards the frequent business traveller and Entre Gold is for the discriminating executive.

L'Hôtel also has the exquisite Chantarelle dining room and one of Toronto's most beautiful garden coffee shops, the Orchard Café, where Philippe Egalon's creations can be seen and eaten daily.

Born in the south of France, Philippe began his apprenticeship at the age of 14. After completing military service, he worked in Paris as a chef for a year and a half. He also worked as a pastry chef on the well-known Côte d'Azur, Riviera and in Nice. When he felt the need for a change, he left Europe for Quebec City, where—as one of the youngest pastry chefs—he worked in some of the top establishments in that city.

Philippe's English improved and he decided to come to Toronto and began work a year and a half ago at L'Hôtel.

L'Hôtel presents a real challenge to young Philippe, who has a staff of nine working under him.

He believes that the key to successful baking is never to cuts corners. He never uses dried or powdered ingredients because they hamper creativity. He has won numerous awards for his sugar work, including a gold and silver medal at the Food and Wine Show.

All of his desserts included are unusual and delicious.

Truffle Cake

Preheat oven to 350°F (180°C).
9" buttered springform (22 cm).

Sponge

4 eggs ³/4 cup sugar (175 ml)	Combine in bowl. Beat for approx. 5 minutes until thick and pale.
¹/3 cup flour (75 ml) 2 tsp cornstarch (10 ml) 4 tbsp cocoa (60 ml)	Sift together and fold into above. Pour into pan and bake for approx. 25-30 minutes, or until tester comes out dry. Cool on rack.

Syrup

¹/2 cup water (125 ml) ¹/4 cup sugar (50 ml)	Boil for 2 minutes. Set aside to cool.

Filling

7 oz. semi-sweet chocolate (200 g)	Melt and set aside.
1 ¹/2 cups whipping cream (375 ml)	Whip until stiff then fold into chocolate until blended.

Assembly

Slice sponge in half lengthwise. Leave bottom half in pan and brush with syrup. Pour in chocolate filling, and refrigerate until firm. (1 hour). Crumble remaining sponge layer over top and decorate sides with toasted almond slices (optional).

Almond Lemon Meringue Tart

Preheat oven to 375°F (190°C).
8-9" buttered flan pan (20-22 cm).

Pastry

4 oz. butter (125 ml) ⎱ ¹/₃ cup sugar (75 ml) ⎰	Cream until light in colour.
2 egg yolks	Add slowly to above mixture.
1 ¹/₄ cups flour (300 ml)	Add and combine until mixture holds together. Use hands. Refrigerate. (If dough is too sticky, add more flour).

Almond Cream

¹/₄ cup butter (50 ml) ⎱ ¹/₄ cup sugar (50 ml) ⎰	Cream until fluffy.
1 egg ⎱ 1 grated rind of lemon ⎰	Add to above and mix.
¹/₄ cup ground almonds (50 ml)	Fold into above.

Put chilled dough into pan, pour almond cream over and then bake 30 minutes or until crust is light brown. Cool on rack. Raise oven to 475°F (240°C).

Lemon Filling

4 egg yolks 4 eggs ¹/₂ cup sugar (125 ml) Juice of 1 ¹/₂ lemons 2 tbsp soft butter (30 ml)	Combine all ingredients in double boiler over low-moderate heat. Do not let water boil. Beat every 5 minutes for 15 minutes until thick. Pour over almond cream.

Meringue

5 egg whites	Whip until half volume.
¹/₂ cup sugar (125 ml)	Add slowly, whipping until stiff. Spread over lemon filling. Put into oven until lightly browned.

Apple Torte with Almond Cream

Preheat oven to 400°F (200°C).
9" buttered flan pan (22 cm).

Apple Filling

4 large green apples — Peel, core, and cut into thin slices. Save one sliced apple for decoration.

2/3 cup sugar (150 ml)
¹/4 cup butter (50 ml) — Add to apples then bring to boil in covered saucepan. Remove lid and cook 3-5 minutes more.

¹/4 cup Calvados or Amaretto liqueur (50ml) — Add to apples and pour onto baking sheet to cool. Meanwhile, prepare pastry.

Pastry

4 oz. butter (125 ml)
¹/3 cup sugar (75 ml) — Cream until fluffy.

2 egg yolks — Add slowly to above or until mixture holds together.

1 ¹/4 cups flour (300 ml) — Add until combined. Use more flour if dough is too sticky. Use hands. Put into pan and bake just until light brown, approx. 10 minutes.

Almond Cream

¹/4 cup butter (50 ml)
¹/4 cup sugar (50 ml) — Cream until fluffy.

1 egg
1 grated rind of lemon — Add to butter and sugar then mix.

¹/4 cup ground almonds (50 ml) — Fold into above mixture. Set aside.

Assembly

Strain apples, save liquid. Pour apples into crust. Pour almond cream over apples. Decorate with sliced apple saved earlier. Brush apples with some of liquid from apples. Sprinkle with a little cinnamon and sugar. Place foil over apples and bake 25 minutes. Remove foil and then bake for 10 more minutes. Cool on rack.

Nougat Mousse with Strawberry Sauce

One 2-cup decorated mold (500 ml).

Serves 4-6
(Recipe can be doubled)

Nougat

$^1/_2$ cup sugar (125 ml)
2 $^1/_2$ tbsp water (37 ml)

Cook until sugar bubbles and thickens, approx. 5 minutes on medium-high heat. Do not let turn brown.

$^1/_3$ cup chopped assorted nuts (hazelnut, almond, pistachio, etc. – 75 ml)

Add and stir until combined nuts become coated like candy. Pour onto greased pan. Cool. Grind into small pieces.

Mousse

1 oz candied fruit (30 ml)

Wash fruit to remove syrup.

$^1/_4$ cup brandy (50 ml)

Soak fruit in brandy.

1 cup whipping cream (250 ml)

Whip until stiff. Place in fridge.

$^1/_2$ package gelatin

Pour some cold water over it, and set aside.

2 egg whites

While whipping egg whites,

$^1/_4$ cup sugar (50 ml)
1 tbsp water (15 ml)

cook over heat until sugar bubbles and thickens, approx. 2 minutes before it turns brown.

1 tbsp sugar (15 ml)

When egg whites reach peak, add this amount of sugar to whites and then add cooked sugar. Beat until blended.

Add gelatin to hot pot where sugar was and melt. Add to whites and whip until cool. Fold whipping cream into nougat, add drained fruit and fold into egg whites. Pour into mold. Freeze for two hours or more until set. To loosen dip into bowl of hot water for approx. 5 seconds. Invert on plate. Keep in freezer and serve with sauce.

Strawberry Sauce

1 cup strawberries
(fresh or frozen) 250 ml)
2 tbsp sugar (30 ml)

Purée

MÖVENPICK®
RESTAURANTS OF SWITZERLAND

SHELLEY BEESTON

Shelley, a native Torontonian, studied graphic arts at a local community college. But her love for baking and pastries led her away from the art field eight years ago and took her into the practical world of desserts.

She has been fortunate to train under five chefs of various nationalities, giving her a wide range of creativity and expertise that she brings to the Mövenpick.

The Mövenpick is originally a Swiss company with over 200 restaurants in Switzerland and Germany, plus two in Toronto. The clientele tends to be tourists and locals, as well as anyone who enjoys the fantastic large plaited desserts for which Mövenpick is so famous.

Shelley, unlike many other chefs, has had the opportunity to work in various aspects of the industry, including restaurants, hotels and bakeries. She has been with the prestigious Yorkville Mövenpick for three years. Recently she was appointed executive pastry chef. Shelley enjoys her position because she is given the opportunity to be innovative. Tasting one of her creations is quite an experience.

Strawberry, Lemon and Raspberry Mousse Paté

9 x 5 x 3" loaf pan (23 x 12 x 7 cm).

3 cups whipping cream (750 ml)	Whip until stiff. Divide into three separate bowls. Set aside.
³/4 cup raspberry purée (fresh or frozen) (175 ml)	If puréeing frozen raspberries, drain excess liquid first.
4 tbsp icing sugar (60 ml)	Add to raspberry purée, mixing well.
2 tsp gelatin (10 ml)	Dissolve according to package. Add to raspberry mixture. Fold into one bowl of whipping cream. Pour into pan.
2 kiwi	Slice and lay half amount on top of raspberry mousse.
2 tbsp lemon juice (30 ml) 3 tbsp icing sugar (45 ml) }	Mix until blended.
1 tsp gelatin (5 ml)	Dissolve according to package and add to lemon mixture. Fold into second bowl of whipping cream. Pour over kiwis. Lay other sliced kiwis over top.
³/4 cup strawberry purée (fresh or frozen) (175 ml) 2 tbsp icing sugar (30 ml) 2 tsp gelatin (10 ml) }	Repeat as with raspberry purée. Pour over kiwis. Cover and refrigerate 3-4 hours.
	Loosen by dipping pan into larger pan of hot water for 5 seconds. Invert.
	Decorate top with fresh raspberries and icing sugar.

Kahlua Cream Dream

Preheat oven to 350°F (180°C).
Line 2 cookie sheets with buttered and floured parchment paper.

6 egg whites	Whip until soft peaks form.
$1/2$ cup sugar (125 ml)	Add and whip until stiff. Set aside.
2 whole eggs 4 egg yolks $1/2$ cup sugar (125 ml)	Whip until light and fluffy, about 3-4 minutes.
3 tbsp flour (45 ml) 3 tsp cocoa (15 ml)	Sift together and fold into whole egg mixture. Set aside.

Using a pastry bag, fill with egg white mixture. Pipe five long rows, 1" wide, with a 1" space in between, down the length of one cookie sheet. Repeat on other sheet, to make ten 1" rows of meringue 1" spaces apart. Rinse pastry bag and fill with cocoa mixture. Fill in 1" spaces on cookie sheet with 5 more rows. Repeat on other sheet. The result is 20 rows of a dark and a white pattern. Bake for 10-15 minutes until golden brown. Cool on rack.

Filling

2 cups whipping ream (500 ml)	Whip until stiff.
1 package gelatin	Dissolve according to package. When melted and slightly cooled, fold into whipping cream.
$1/2$ cup Kahlua or coffee liqueur (125 ml)	Fold gently into whipping cream mixture.

Assembly

Invert cookie sheets on clean tea towels dusted with icing sugar. Carefully peel off parchment paper. Cut each large sheet lengthwise into two sections to make four small cakes. Layer with filling and ice entire layer cake with remainder of filling. Decorate with chocolate shavings.

Patachou

CHRISTIAN SEREBECBERE

Christian was born into the food business in France. His father owned three hotels and was himself an executive chef. But it was in England that Christian formally studied cooking.

It was while visiting Canada that Christian fell in love with this country and made plans to move here. First it was Montreal and then he moved to Toronto, where he worked at the Inn on the Park for two years. Following that, he was at the Napoleon Restaurant and the Harbour Castle as sous chef. But it was while working at Maison Basque that Christian developed a love for pastry. And nine years ago, when he received an offer from Patachou, he just couldn't refuse.

Featuring French pastry, Patachou has two successful locations in Toronto. The original store is at Bathurst and Eglinton. Seven years ago the Yonge Street bakery opened.

Christian, who has 14 people working with him, believes that Toronto has grown up dramatically in the past ten years and is now a dessert haven. He feels we're world-class, on a par with the greatest American and European cities.

Chocolate is still Toronto's first love, Christian says. The hint he gives to bakers is, if you want the best results, always use good ingredients and never take short-cuts. Christian provided us with some very special desserts from among the best of his classical French creations. An easy Gâteau St. Honoré is among his selection.

Tarte Tartin
(Upside down apple tart
made with Phyllo)

Preheat oven to 350°F (180°C).
9 or 10" pie pan completely lined with foil (22-25 cm). Butter only foiled sides of pan.

7 small-medium Granny Smith apples	Peel. core, and slice each apple into 6 pieces. Set aside.
3 tbsp butter (45 ml) } $^1/_3$ cup sugar (75 ml) }	Place in saucepan until butter is melted. Set aside.
$1^1/_2$ tbsp sugar (22 ml) } $^1/_2$ tbsp cinnamon (7 ml) }	Mix. Set aside.
4 tbsp soft butter (60 ml)	Spread butter over foil in pan until evenly distributed. Place apple slices on sides and bottom of pan. Sprinkle with cinnamon mixture. Pour melted butter/ sugar mixture over apples.
8 sheets of phyllo	Fold each sheet in half and lay over apples. Tuck edges in after each sheet. Brush top sheet with butter. Bake approx. 30 minutes until golden brown. Cool on rack approx. 2 hours. Cover tart with serving plate and invert quickly. Excess liquid can be absorbed with paper towels.

Best if served immediately.

Gâteau Saint Honoré
(Puff pastry filled with pastry cream)

Preheat oven to 400°F (200°C).
Large buttered and floured cookie sheet.

Pastry

1/2 cup water (125 ml) 1/2 tsp salt (2 ml) 2 oz. butter (60 ml)	Put into saucepan and bring to a boil. Remove from heat.
1/3 cup flour (75 ml)	Add, mixing well. Bring back to a medium heat, stirring vigorously for a minute or two until pastry comes away from saucepan. Remove from heat, stirring vigorously again.
3 medium eggs	Add one at a time, and whisk well until combined. Cover bowl with cloth.

Spoon or pipe pastry onto sheet in the size of walnuts. Sprinkle with some sugar and bake 20-25 minutes, until golden brown. (Do not open door for first 15 minutes). Cool on rack.

Pastry Cream

1 cup milk (250 ml) 1/2 tsp vanilla (2 ml)	Boil in saucepan. Lower heat.
1/4 cup sugar (50 ml) 1 egg	In clean bowl, mix well.
2 tbsp flour (30 ml)	Add to egg mixture, blending well.

Pour half of the hot milk into egg mixture, and then pour back into remainder of milk. Stir on low-medium heat until thickened. Beat until smooth. Pour into bowl, cover top of pastry cream with plastic wrap and chill.

Gâteau Saint Honoré
– Puff pastry filled with pastry cream –
(continued)

1 cup whipping cream (250 ml)	Whip until firm.
1 1/2 tbsp kirsch liqueur (22 ml)	Add and blend gently. Fold 1/3 of whipped cream into cooled pastry cream. Save remainder.

Cut a small hole into bottom of puffs. Using a spoon or pastry bag, fill with pastry cream. Place on serving dish in a circular fashion. Spoon remaining 2/3 whipping cream into centre. Decorate puff tops with chocolate sauce (bottled), or caramelized sugar, (below).

Caramelized Sugar

1/2 cup sugar (125 ml) 2 tbsp water (30 ml)	Place over medium heat and stir.
3 drops lemon juice	Before boiling, add. Let mixture turn a light golden brown, while stirring occasionally, about 5 minutes. Remove from heat. Do not let sugar turn dark brown. Carefully spoon over puffs.
	Serve the same day.

Plum Tart Patachou

Preheat oven to 375°F (190°C)
9-10" tart pan (22-25 cm)

Pastry

^{1}/2 cup butter (125 ml) ⎫
  ^{1}/3 cup sugar (75 ml) ⎭   Cream until blended.

           1 egg ⎫
1 tsp vanilla (5 ml) ⎭   Add to above mixture and blend.

1 ^{1}/4 cup flour (300 ml)   Stir into above ingredients until mixture holds together. If too sticky, add more flour. If too dry, add a little icewater. Chill in plastic for 30 minutes. Meanwhile, prepare plums.

Filling

^{1}/2 cup butter (125 ml)   Melt in large saucepan.

^{1}/2 cup sugar (125ml)   Combine until blended.

2 tbsp cognac (30 ml)   Add 1 tbsp (15 ml) and bring to boil.

2 lbs pitted ripe plums (1 kg)   Slice in half and add to above. Reduce heat and cook covered 5 minutes. Add remaining cognac. Cool in refrigerator.

Pat dough into pan. Bake until golden brown 15-20 minutes. Spoon plums and juice into crust. Increase heat to 450°F (230°C) and bake 5 minutes longer. Do not refrigerate tart. Keep out at room temperature.

MAX WIRTH

Paul's French Foods is a landmark in Toronto's exclusive Forest Hill area. Since opening in the 1950's, this shop has always ranked among the best as both a caterer to many cities in Ontario and as the source of some of the finest desserts in this city.

Max Wirth, the pastry chef, was born in Switzerland. He did his training near Zurich and worked for many exclusive European hotels and bakeries before coming to Toronto in the early 1950's.

Max met the original Paul when he arrived and worked for years at Chez Charbon. Two years ago he came to Paul's French Foods, directing the creation of desserts. Max sets very high standards and feels that this is why Paul's remains so successful, even after 30 years. Paul's truffle cake and mousse cake have always been favourites and, luckily, he has shared both recipes with us, as well as other delicacies.

His belief is that simplicity has almost disappeared and that today's cakes have too many "gimmicks" to make them delicious. Paul's, synonymous with quality, sticks to the basics, which keeps their customers coming back. You'll discover why when you prepare the wide variety of desserts shown here.

Buttercream Sponge Mousse Cake

Preheat oven to 425°F (220°C).
3 8" buttered and floured pans lined with parchment paper (20 cm).

Sponge

5 egg yolks 3 tbsp sugar (45 ml) }	Whip for 2 minutes until thick and pale.
1 tbsp soft butter (15 ml)	Beat in above mixture and blend.
2 tbsp flour (30 ml) 2 tbsp finely ground almonds (30 ml) }	Fold in gently.
3 egg whites 3 tbsp sugar (45 ml) }	Whip until stiff. Fold quickly into batter. Pour in 3 pans and bake approx. 5 minutes or until tester comes out clean.

Buttercream

* 3/4 cup soft butter (room temperature) (175 ml) 1/2 cup icing sugar (125 ml) }	Whip until light.
* 2 egg whites (must be room temp)	Heat egg whites in double boiler on low heat until lukewarm to touch. Do not overcook.
1 tbsp instant coffee dissolved in a little hot water (15 ml)	Add to whites, mix and then add to above butter and sugar mixture. Whip until blended.

Brush sponge layer with liqueur of choice and layer with buttercream. Refrigerate.

* Butter and whites should be taken out 2 hours before being used. Buttercream will not combine unless butter is soft and whites slightly warm.

Buttercream Sponge Mousse Cream
(continued)

Mousse

12 oz semisweet chocolate (375 g)	Melt.
$3/4$ cup 10% cream (175 ml)	Add slowly to above until blended.
1 $1/2$ cups whipping cream (375 ml)	Whip until stiff. Fold in $2/3$ of chocolate mixture. Reserve other third.

Pour two-thirds of the cream chocolate mixture on top and sides of cake, and spread. Refrigerate until set. Glaze top and sides of cake with remaining one-third of chocolate mixture.

Hazelnut Layered Truffle Cake

Preheat oven to 350°F (180°C).
Two 8" well-buttered and floured springform pans (22 cm) or 2 round pans lined with buttered parchment.

Chocolate Sponge

2 oz butter (60 ml)
2 oz semisweet chocolate (60 g) } Melt, mix and set aside.

8 egg yolks
4 tbsp sugar (60 ml) } Whip until thick and pale. Add melted chocolate, mixing well.

4 tbsp flour (60 ml)
4 tbsp ground hazelnuts (60 ml) } Fold gently into egg/sugar mixture.

8 egg whites
4 tbsp sugar (60 ml) } Beat until stiff. Fold gently into above. Pour into pans, bake for 20 minutes or until tester comes out clean. Cool on rack.

Truffle Filling

20 oz semisweet chocolate (375 g) Melt.

10 oz 10% cream (300 ml)
2 tsp vanilla (10 ml) Slowly add to above. Cool slightly, then whip lightly.

Refrigerate to obtain proper spreading consistency.

Assembly

Slice two sponge cakes lengthwise to yield 4 sponge cakes. Layer with filling between, saving enough for tops and sides. Refrigerate until set before glazing tops and sides.

Lemon Cream Mousse

4 individual serving bowls or
1 decorated glass bowl, or 2 cup mold.

Recipe can be doubled.

Juice of 2 medium sized lemons
Grated rind of 1 lemon
$^1/_4$ cup butter (50 ml)
$^1/_3$ cup sugar (75 ml)

Combine in double boiler and bring to a boil. Turn stove to lowest heat after 3 minutes.

2 whole eggs

Beat eggs in clean bowl and pour some of above mixture into eggs, mix and pour back into remaining lemon mixture.

On low heat stir until mixture slightly thickens, approx. 5-7 minutes. If heat is too high eggs will curdle. Remove from heat.

$^1/_2$ package gelatin

Dissolve according to package and when melted add to above.

Cool mixture completely before continuing.

1 cup whipping cream (250 ml)

Whip until close to stiff.

2 egg whites

In separate bowl whip until half volume reached.

$^1/_4$ cup sugar (50 ml)

Add and beat until almost stiff.

Only when lemon mixture is completely cooled, fold in whipping cream and then egg whites, until combined. Pour into bowls and chill 2-4 hours.

Wine Cream Mousse

4-5 individual glass bowls or
1 larger glass bowl.

4 egg yolks
1/2 cup sugar (125 ml) } Beat until pale and thick.

1 tbsp cornstarch (15 ml) — Add to above mixing well. Set aside.

1 cup white wine (250 ml)
juice of 1/2 orange
juice of 1/2 lemon } In saucepan boil to reduce by half, approx. 10 minutes. Pour slowly into yolk mixture, mix and then pour back into pot on stove and cook on low heat until mixture is thick enough to coat a spoon. Cool. Stir occasionally.

1/2 package gelatin — Dissolve according to package and stir into above.

2 egg whites — Beat until half volume.

2 tbsp sugar (30 ml) — Slowly add, beating until stiff. Fold into wine mixture (when cool). Pour into glasses. Refrigerate until set, 2-4 hours.

Incredibly sophisticated!

▷

L'Hôtel

Truffle Cake
(ribbon – a sugar creation
by Philippe Egalon)

Crème Caramel

Preheat oven to 325°F (160°C).
5-8 individual baking cups (depending on size).

1/2 cup sugar (125 ml)	Melt in pot with a few drops of lemon juice. Pour into cups coating bottom and sides.
2 cups milk (500 ml)	Scald in clean pot.
1/2 cup sugar (125 ml) 3 eggs 2 egg yolks 1/2 tsp vanilla (2 ml) grated rind of 1/2 orange	Mix in bowl with spoon. Pour hot milk into egg mixture slowly. Stir well. Fill cups and bake in a large pan filled with water (bain-marie) for 40-50 minutes or until mixture appears firm.
	Cool, refrigerate and then run knife around edges before inverting. Decorate with fresh fruit or whipped cream.

An old-time favourite!

◁

Sutton Place

Raspberry Pyramid with crème anglaise

HOTEL

BRIAN MORIN

For 20 years Sutton Place has been a home away from home for TV and motion picture stars as well as businessmen. Right in the heart of downtown Toronto, Sutton Place is known for its magnificent Sanssouci and the famous Chef's Table. Both dining rooms are charmingly European, reflecting the elegance of Louis XIV and Louis XV.

Brian Morin is one of the few pastry chefs featured in *The Dessert Scene* who is a Torontonian. All his life he has loved food and wanted to be a chef, despite the fact that no one else in his family had similar aspirations.

He trained locally in culinary management, then gained experience in a CP hotel in Nova Scotia, the Napoleon Restaurant in Toronto, the Four Seasons Hotel in Yorkville, and, finally, last year joined the Sutton Place Hotel.

Brian strongly believes that Toronto is now a leader in food trends due to the many nationalities which make up our cosmopolitan city. As far as desserts are concerned, he feels the most important element is that *everything* must be fresh and, if bakers want to grow and be creative, they should have a good understanding of the basics – "how a dough works" – which will ultimately lead to new ideas. He takes pride in stating that all desserts at the Sutton Place are made from scratch.

Brian's speciality and first love is plaited desserts, of which he is justifiably proud. Each plaited dessert requires incredible artistry and, when 200 are ordered, each must be magnificent. He also loves preparing soufflés, which he feels are making a comeback. He features his classic Grand Marnier Soufflé in *The Dessert Scene*.

While he's not sure what the future has in store, Brian hopes someday to operate his own café or work as an executive chef at the hotel, overseeing the entire operation. His talents are apparent in his desserts, which can be characterised as elegant yet simple.

Chocolate Success Cake

Preheat oven to 350°F (180°C).
9" buttered and floured springform (22 cm).

12 oz semi-sweet chocolate (375 g) 1 tbsp dry instant coffee (15 ml) 1/4 cup rum or chocolate liqueur (50 ml) 2 tbsp vanilla (30 ml) 1/4 cup hot water (50 ml)	Melt together in large bowl. Set aside.
6 eggs 1/2 cup sugar (125 ml)	Whip until light, approx. 2-3 minutes. Fold into chocolate mixture.
1 cup whipping cream (250 ml)	Whip until stiff. Fold into other ingredients until blended.

Pour into pan and bake one hour, then lower temperature to 250°F (120°C) for 1/2 hour. Bake in middle of oven with pan of water on rack below for extra moisture. Cake falls like souffle. Cool on rack and decorate with icing sugar or piped whipped cream.

A chocolate success every time!

"Classic" Grand Marnier Soufflé

Preheat oven to 400°F (200°C)
4 individual molds buttered and sprinkled with sugar or
1 large 4-5 cup mold (1 l.)

1/2 cup milk (125 ml)	Heat in saucepan.
1 3/4 tbsp butter (26 ml)	In another saucepan melt butter.
1 3/4 tbsp flour (26 ml)	Add to butter until dough forms. Pour in heated milk and bring to a boil (1-2 minutes).
3 tbsp Grand Marnier (45 ml) ⎫ 2 egg yolks ⎭	Add to other ingredients and mix well. Put mixture aside until dessert is to be served.
	* Make crème anglaise (optional) before completing soufflé.

* The above may be prepared ahead of time. The finishing step is the whipped egg whites, only to be completed just before it goes into the oven.

4 egg whites	Whip until half volume reached.
1/3 cup sugar (75 ml)	Add half of this sugar. Beat until mixed, not long. Fold in remaining half of sugar. Fold into above milk/flour mixture. Pour into mold and bake 20 minutes in bain-marie pan filled with hot water. Do not open oven during first 15 minutes of baking. Top should be browned and inflated.
	Serve with crème anglaise (optional).

"Classic" Grand Marnier Soufflé
(continued)

Crème Anglaise

1 cup milk (250 ml)	Heat in saucepan.
2 tbsp sugar (30 ml) ⎫ 3 egg yolks ⎬ $^1/_2$ tsp vanilla (2 ml) ⎭	Whisk in bowl until light. Pour some hot milk into eggs, mix and then pour back into milk and cook on low heat until mixture coats back of spoon. Do not boil.
	Cool before serving.

*So easy, you'll wonder why
you didn't make more soufflés before.*

Raspberry Pyramid
(pistachio wafers
with raspberries and cream)

Preheat oven to 425°F (220°C)
Butter and flour 2 large cookie sheets. 6 servings or more

Pistachio Mixture

1 oz honey (30 ml) 1/2 cup icing sugar (125 ml) 4 large egg whites 1 cup scant flour (250 ml)	Mix in bowl until blended.
1 1/4 oz hot melted butter (38 ml)	Add and mix well.
1 oz finely chopped pistaccios (30 ml)	Add and blend.

Take 2 tsp (10 ml) of mixture and, with a knife, spread to a width of approx. 3" (7.5 cm), so thin as to almost be transparent. The thinness is a crucial step to get the light wafer desired. Place as many on the cookie sheet as will fit. Bake for 5 minutes until the edges are brown. Cool on rack until crisp. Grease and flour sheet again and repeat. Four wafers make one dessert, therefore if serving 6, make 24 wafers. Refrigerate any remaining dough. Can be used at a later date.

Crème Anglaise

1 cup milk (250 ml)	Heat in saucepan until simmering. Lower heat.
2 tbsp sugar (30 ml) 3 egg yolks	Whisk together in bowl until light.
1/2 tsp milk (2 ml)	Add to sugar mixture. Pour some milk into eggs, blend and pour blended mixture back into milk. Stir or beat on low heat until thickened. Do not let boil. Cool.

Raspberry Pyramid
(pistachio wafers with raspberries and cream)

Cream and Raspberries

1 cup whipping cream (250 ml)
1 tbsp icing sugar (15 ml) } Whip until stiff. Set aside.

1 pint fresh raspberries

Assembly

Place some crème anglaise on individual serving dish. Place wafer on sauce, add some whipped cream on top of each wafer, then some raspberries over cream. Finish with a dot of whipped cream and another wafer. Repeat using a total of four wafers. (Top layer is wafer, sprinkled with icing sugar and chopped pistachios). Repeat for number of servings desired.

Note:

If additional raspberry decoration is desired on crème anglaise, purée some raspberries and, with a knife, marble it through the crème anglaise. Also, any assortment of berries is possible.

Maple Pecan Tart

Preheat oven to 375°F (190°C)
9-10" tart pan (25 cm)

Sweet Pastry

$^1/_2$ cup soft butter (125 ml)
$^1/_4$ cup sugar (50 ml)

Beat until mixed and creamy.

$^1/_2$ tsp vanilla (2 ml)
$^1/_2$ beaten egg
pinch salt
$^1/_2$ tbsp milk (7 ml)

Blend into above.

1 $^1/_2$ cup flour (375 ml)
$^1/_3$ cup ground almonds (75 ml)

Fold into above until firm and mixture holds together. Put into bottom and sides of pan and prebake until light brown, approx. 15-20 minutes. Cool on rack. Lower heat to 325°F (160°C).

Maple Mixture

$^2/_3$ cup maple syrup (150 ml)
$^1/_2$ cup sugar (125 ml)

Heat in saucepan until sugar dissolves. Remove from heat.

3 eggs
2 tbsp butter (30 ml)
1 $^1/_2$ cups half or chopped pecans (375 ml)

Add and mix well. Pour mixture into crust and bake 20-30 minutes or until firm to touch.

The maple creates a very different type of pecan pie!

Old Fashioned Pots of Chocolate

Preheat oven to 325°F (160°C)
5-6 individual oven proof bowls.

1 cup milk (250 ml) 1 cup whipping cream (250 ml)	Heat in saucepan until hot.
3 oz semisweet chocolate (85 g)	Add to milk and cream, stirring until melted.
5 egg yolks 1/4 cup sugar (50 ml) 1/4 tsp vanilla (1 ml)	Beat in clean bowl until fluffy. Add some hot milk mixture to eggs, blend and pour back into remaining milk mixture. Blend. Remove from heat.

Pour into bowls and then place in large pan filled with water (bain-marie). Bake for 45 minutes. Mixture looks unset, but chocolate firms later. Chill until ready to serve.

Spiced Poached Pears
with Sabayon Sauce

3 cups red wine (750 ml)
1 1/4 cup sugar (300 ml)
1 cinnamon stick
3 cloves
1 orange cut into quarters
1 lemon cut into quarters

Bring to boil in large pot.
Lower heat.

6 pears

Peel, core, and cut in half then add to wine. Simmer 15-20 minutes until pears are tender when knife inserted. Cool in juice. The longer the pears rest in juice, the better the taste. But they can be served as soon as they are cold.

Sabayon Sauce

1 cup white wine (250 ml)
4 egg yolks
2 whole eggs
1/2 cup sugar (125 ml)

Blend well in double boiler over simmering heat. Whip until mixture becomes light coloured and slightly thickened, approx. 3-5 minutes. Remove from heat and continue beating for a couple of minutes.
Serve pears on top of sauce.

Sweet Sue Pastries

SUE DEVOR

It's a tradition at Sweet Sue's to stop before the store window and look at the unusual mannequins. And once you're inside, you'll be astounded again, this time by the decadent and artistic desserts in the show cases, all of which are utterly delicious.

Sue has always loved working with food, even when she was raising her five children. She began baking in her home for restaurants and became so successful that three years ago she opened her first location at Eglinton and Bathurst. Recently she opened a second at the suburban Promenade Mall.

Encompassing a wide clientèle, Sue caters to the wholesale and retail trade as well as a corporate market. Her corporate work involves designing such items as a mountain cake with a train going through it for the opening of Canada's Wonderland.

Sue has travelled all over the United States and Europe and finds that Toronto is on a par with other big cities. Her success, she believes, is due to using good quality ingredients and never losing her creativity. She refuses to rely exclusively on her twenty different varieties of desserts but constantly creates new ones by staying aware of what people like.

To assure success, Sue advises home bakers to use natural high-quality ingredients, know your oven well and stick to simple desserts which you have the confidence and ability to prepare.

In the years to come, Sue hopes to expand her operations to more and more suburban locations because she believes that's where the demand is. In the meantime, enjoy Sweet Sue's delicacies.

Strawberry Kiwi Cream Cheese Chocolate Flan

Preheat oven to 375°F (190°C).
9-10"removeable flan pan (22-25 cm).

Crust

1 1/2 cups flour (375 ml) 1/4 cup sugar (50 ml)	Combine.
3/4 cup butter (175 ml)	Cut into dry ingredients until crumbly.
1 1/2 tsp white vinegar (6 ml)	Add until dough is well combined. Let rest 30 minutes. Press into pan and chill 5-10 minutes in freezer. Bake 15-20 minutes or until lightly brown. Cool on rack.

Filling

2 oz semisweet chocolate (55 g)	Melt.
1 tbsp whipping cream (15 ml)	Add to above, mix and then pour into crust. Chill a few minutes.
1/2 lb cream cheese (250 g) 3 tbsp icing sugar (45 ml) 1-2 tbsp milk (15-30 ml) 1/4 tsp vanilla (1 ml)	Combine and mix until smooth. Spread over chocolate. Chill a few minutes.

Topping

Decorate with combination of sliced strawberries and kiwis. Glaze with 2 tbsp (30 ml) of apple or red currant jelly.

The combination of fruit, cream cheese and chocolate is extraordinary!

Chocolate Torte

Preheat oven to 350°F (180°C)
2 8 or 9" round buttered and floured cake pans. (20-22 cm).

Cake

1 3/4 cups flour (425 ml)
1 3/4 cup sugar (425 ml)
3/4 cup cocoa (175 ml)
1 1/4 tsp baking soda (6 ml)
1 1/2 tsp baking powder (7 ml)
1/2 tsp salt (2 ml)
} Sift together in large bowl.

1/4 cup soft butter (50 ml)
1/2 cup oil (125 ml)
1 1/4 cup warm milk (300 ml)
1 tsp vanilla (5 ml)
} Add to above and beat at medium speed for 2 minutes, scraping bowl.

3 eggs

Add and beat for 2 more minutes. Pour into pans and bake 25-30 minutes or until tester comes out clean. Cool on rack before turning out of pans.

Chocolate Cream Filling & Icing

4 cups whipping cream (1 l.)
1 package whipping cream stabilizer (optional)
} Whip until soft.

2/3 cup chocolate syrup (name brand) (150 ml)
1-2 tbsp coffee liqueur or rum (15-30 ml)
} Add to above and beat until stiff.

Assembly

Level tops of cakes with sharp knife. Carefully split lengthwise both cakes into three layers each, totalling 6 layers. Place one layer on dish, spread with cream , and then repeat until all layers are iced. Frost entire cake with icing. Garnish with chocolate curls, toasted almonds and chocolate dipped strawberries.

One of Sweet Sue's most beautiful to serve!

Easy Coffee Cake

Preheat oven to 350°F (180°C)
8" buttered and floured square pan (22 cm).

Topping

> 1/2 cup brown sugar (125 ml)
> 2 tsp cinnamon (10 ml)
> 3 tbsp flour (45 ml)
> 1 1/2 tbsp oil (22 ml)
> 1 tbsp chopped nuts (15 ml)
> 1/2 cup chocolate chips (optional) (125 ml)

Mix together until crumbly. Set aside.

Cake

> 2 eggs
> 1 cup sugar (250 ml)
> 1 tsp vanilla (5 ml)

Beat in bowl until fluffy.

> 1 1/3 cups flour (325 ml)
> 1 1/2 tsp baking powder (6 ml)
> pinch salt

In separate bowl sift together.

> 1/2 cup oil (125 ml)
> 6 tbsp orange juice or milk (90 ml)

In small bowl combine. Add alternatively with dry ingredients to egg mixture, just until combined.

Pour half the batter into pan. Sprinkle on half the topping, and then pour on remaining batter. Then sprinkle with remaining topping. Bake for 30-40 miniutes or until toothpick comes out clean. Cool on rack.

ELIZABETH VOLGYESI AND SUZY OKUN

Elizabeth Volgyesi and Suzy Okun, two friends, started their careers by making truffles at home for posh restaurants and stores in Toronto. A year after they began they realized how limited that market is and decided to try something different.

Suzy observed that everywhere that good food is sold and served the baker or chef is "the hidden wonder" in the backroom. They decided to change that concept by putting the bakers upfront where customers can see them, making the customer a participant in the creative process.

In 1977 the first Treats opened on Bloor Street in the centre of Toronto's most prestigious shopping strip. Immediately line-ups formed outside their small store, customers seduced by the sight, smell and assured quality of the fresh and wholesome cookies for sale.

Treats was one of the first stores to give cookies a personality by offering huge cookies in different shapes and letting customers add a personalized message. After this successful idea, Treats expanded, developing fifty different flavours of muffins. By 1980 Treats had become so popular that today it is a major franchised chain operation with over sixty stores across Canada.

Treats has always featured quality, cleanliness and quick, nutritious snacks, evident at every outlet. Elizabeth has taken us back to 1977 and shared some of the initial recipes that Treats offered.

Coffee Truffles

About 24 truffles

$^1/_2$ lb semi-sweet chocolate (250 g)

Melt.

$^3/_4$ cup icing sugar (175 ml)
$^3/_4$ cup roasted ground almonds (175 g)
1 oz soft butter (30 ml)
1 tbsp coffee (or to taste) (15 ml)

Add to chocolate mixing with a wooden spoon until spoon. Refrigerate until hard enough to roll into balls.

When firm, roll into small balls. Then roll in cocoa, icing sugar and/or chopped toasted nuts. Store in a cool place.

Sweet Sue Pastries

Strawberry and Kiwi
Cream Cheese Chocolate Flan

Chocolate Chip Nut Brownies with White Chocolate Glaze

Preheat oven to 350°F (180°C).
8" buttered and floured square pan. (20 cm).

1/3 cup semisweet chocolate (75 g) 1/2 cup butter (125 ml) }	Melt, blend and cool.
2 eggs 3/4 cup sugar (175 ml) 1/4 tsp salt 1 tbsp vanilla (15 ml) }	Whisk until mixed. Add melted chocolate mixture and blend well.
1/2 cup flour (125 ml)	Fold in just until combined.
1 1/2 oz chocolate chips (45 g) 1 1/2 oz chopped nuts (45 ml) }	Fold in gently.
	Pour into pan and bake approx. 20-25 minutes or until centre remains a little moist. Do not allow batter to become dry.
	Place on rack while preparing icing.

Glaze

3 oz white chocolate (85 g)	Melt and then glaze brownies. Let cool until set.

*The white chocolate topping
gives these brownies their uniqueness.*

◁

Dessert Peddler

Carrot Cake

PASTRY CHEF – NORBERT MAUSHAGEN

Comfortably nestled on St. Thomas Street in Toronto's fashionable Bay/Bloor area is the Windsor Arms, a small, elegant and private hotel in the European tradition.

The Windsor Arms is proud to be a member of the exclusive Paris-based association of hotels and restaurants, Relais et Châteaux. The hotel is equally proud to have Norbert Maushagen as their pastry chef.

Norbert, born in Germany, decided at a young age to pursue the life of a pastry chef. He spent three and a half years apprenticing and another five years earning his Masters, the highest degree attainable in pastry. After his education, he worked at the Hilton in Dusseldorf and the Savoy in London. In 1976, while attending the Olympics in Montreal, he became so enchanted with Canada that he decided to make it his home.

His work in Toronto began at the Four Seasons in Yorkville, continued at the exclusive L'Hotel, then on to the lakefront Harbour Castle Hilton and ultimately the Windsor Arms. Norbert needs to feel creative, which he believes is what keeps his desserts looking and tasting among the best in the city, and will move to another venue to meet his own rigorous standards.

He believes that ten years ago Toronto's dessert industry was unsophisticated but that today our standards are as high as those in Europe.

Sugar and chocolate desserts, almost everyone's favourites, are Norbert's specialties. He feels that expert pastry chefs cannot be compared with one another, they simply have different tastes.

His main hint to the average baker is that an exquisite decoration is not as important as the essential recipe and ingredients. Any dessert can always look beautiful. But only if the basics are consistent and of the highest quality will a dessert be wonderfully memorable. His specialties given to the book include some of the best parfaits ever created. Bon appetit!

Cointreau Chocolate Cream
with Meringue

Preheat oven to 350°F (180°C).
9" springform (20 cm).
3 cookie sheets lined with buttered parchment paper
(draw three 9" circles (22 cm) on each sheet).

Meringue

6 egg whites	Whip until stiff peaks form.
1 cup sugar (250 ml)	Add slowly, beating until stiff.
1 cup ground hazelnuts (250 ml) } 1/4 cup flour (50 ml) }	Fold in gently.

With pastry bag or spoon, fill in 3 circles on cookie sheets with
meringue. Bake for 10 minutes. Cool on rack.

Filling

3 cups whipping cream (750 ml) } 3/4 cup sugar (175 ml) }	Whip until stiff. Divide into two bowls.
1/3 cup chocolate (75 g) } 2 tbsp Cointreau (orange liqueur) (30 ml) }	Melt and cool. Add to one of the above bowls. Blend well.
1/2 cup chopped toasted almonds (125 ml) 1/2 cup chopped toasted filberts (125 ml) 1/2 cup chocolate chips (125 g) }	Mix together then add to other bowl of whipping cream.

Assembly

Place one meringue in springform. Add chocolate chip, nut mixture. Add
another meringue. Add Cointreau mixture. Add third meringue.
Refrigerate until cold. Decorate with icing sugar and chocolate
shavings.

Kahlua Freeze

Preheat oven to 400°F (200°C).
8" springform pan (20 cm). Butter and sprinkle with dry bread crumbs.

Sponge

5 eggs ²/₃ cup sugar (150 ml) }	Whisk until stiff, about 5 minutes.
¹/₃ cup flour (75 ml) ¹/₃ cup cocoa (75 ml) }	Fold into eggs. Pour into pan and bake approx. 20-25 minutes or until tester comes out dry.
	Cool on rack. When cool, slice cake into 2 layers, lengthwise. Leave one in pan and carefully remove the other a plate dusted with icing sugar.

Kahlua Parfait

6 egg yolks ³/₄ cup sugar (175 ml) }	Whisk until light and creamy and until sugar is dissolved.
4 tbsp Kahlua (60 ml)	Add and mix.
2 cups whipping cream (500 ml)	In a separate bowl beat until stiff and then fold into egg mixture. Pour onto sponge layer in a pan. Carefully top with second sponge layer. Freeze 3-4 hours or until set.

Kahlua Freeze
(continued)

Optional Vanilla and Chocolate Sauces – Cake is delicious on its own.

Vanilla Sauce

2 cups milk (500 ml)	Bring almost to a boil. Turn heat to low.
5 egg yolks ⎱ 1/4 cup sugar (50 ml) ⎰	Mix well, adding a little milk to eggs. Mix and pour back into remaining milk. Heat until thick. Do not let boil.
1 tsp vanilla (5 ml)	Add and remove from heat. Divide mixture in half.

Kahlua Sauce

4 oz semisweet chocolate (125 g) ⎱ 2 tbsp Kahlua (30 ml) ⎰	Dissolve in half of above sauce and beat until combined.

Serve parfait with vanilla and chocolate sauce on both sides.

Peach Freeze

2 cup mold (500 ml) or 4 individual molds

Serves 4
Recipe can be doubled.

Parfait

³/4 cup sugar (175 ml) }
10 egg yolks }
Beat until light and creamy. Set aside.

1 cup whipping cream (250 ml)
Whip until stiff then fold into above.

¹/3 cup Peach schnapps (75 ml) }
juice of ¹/4 lemon }
Add to above. Pour into mold and freeze until set (2-4 hours).

Loosen by placing in pan of hot water for 5-10 seconds and invert carefully onto serving dish. Sometimes a few more seconds are necessary. Do not keep in hot water for too long or parfait will melt. Freeze until ready to serve.

Peach sauce

¹/2 cup puréed canned or fresh }
peaches (125 ml) }
1 tbsp icing sugar (15 ml) }
1 tsp peach liqueur (5 ml) }
Combine and serve with parfait.

Hazelnut Parfait with Chocolate Sauce

One 9 x 5 x 3" loaf pan (23 x 12 x 7 cm).   Recipe can be cut in half.

5 egg yolks
2 eggs
³/₄ cup sugar (175 ml)

Beat until stiff. Divide into two separate bowls.

¹/₂ cup ground toasted hazelnuts (125 ml)

Add to one bowl.

4 oz. milk chocolate (125 g)

Melt and cool. Set aside.

2 ¹/₂ cups whipping cream (625 ml)

Whip until stiff.

Fold into milk chocolate. Add to other bowl of egg mixture without the nuts.

Add nut filling to pan, level, then add chocolate filling on top. Freeze until set (2-3 hours). Loosen by dipping pan into larger bowl of hot water for 5-10 seconds. Invert onto serving dish. (If mold needs more time, only give a few seconds of the parfait will melt). Freeze.

Chocolate Sauce

2 ¹/₂ oz semi-sweet chocolate (75 g)

Melt.

³/₄ cup whipping cream (175 ml)
1 ¹/₂ tbsp nut liqueur (optional) (22 ml)

Add gradually and blend.

Cool. Serve alongside pieces of parfait.

Just like heavenly ice cream, but easier to make.

JOHN MATHESON AND BOB DUNCAN

John Matheson and Bob Duncan, owners of Thames Valley Antiques, have always been ice cream addicts. They were convinced that Toronto needed a sophisticated old-time ice cream parlour not only to remind us of the ones from the 1900s but also to sell an incredible variety of quality of ice cream. In 1984 W.D. Kones was born and now has three central locations in the city.

John and Bob have a philosophy: to deliver fresh and pure ice cream in as many as 18 flavours in one day, including such exotic treats as Irish cream, chocolate raspberry and mango. W.D. Kones total repertoire includes 40 different flavours.

Recently they entered the world of sorbets and ices and have attracted orders from some of Toronto's finest hotel and dining establishments.

Go ahead and get into making your own ice cream. It's well worth the effort.

Oreo Cookies and Cream

4 egg yolks
$^1/_2$ cup sugar (125 ml)
1 tsp vanilla (5 ml)
1 cup half and half (250 ml)

Whip until mixed. Place over double boiler under medium heat and beat until double in volume, approx. 5-7 minutes.

Remove from heat. Let pot cool in a pan of cold water.

1 $^3/_4$ cups whipping cream (425 ml)

Add into above when cool, and blend. Pour into ice cream machine and freeze according to manufacturer's instructions.

1 $^1/_3$ cup coarsely broken Oreo cookies (325 ml)

When ice cream is half-frozen, mix in cookies and freeze until ready.

To soften before serving, remove from freezer and place in refrigerator for half an hour.

Not just for kids!

Chocolate Raspberry Ice Cream

1 cup raspberries
(fresh or frozen)(250 ml)
1/2 cup sugar (125 ml)

In double boiler, heat until fruit becomes soft, about 10 minutes. Purée and chill while making ice cream.

4 egg yolks
1/3 cup sugar (75 ml)
1 cup half and half (250 ml)

Combine in double boiler over medium heat and beat for approx. 5-7 minutes until double in volume.

5 oz. semisweet chocolate
(140 g)

Melt and add to above. Continue beating until combined.

Set bowl in large pan of cool water to chill (10 minutes).

1 1/2 cups whipping cream
(375 ml)

When chocolate mixture is cool, pour in cream and mix well. Pour into ice cream freezer according to manufacturer's instructions. When half-frozen, pour in raspberry mixture and then continue chilling until ice cream is ready.

What a combination!
Only W.D. Kones could have discovered this.

Mango Sundae

6-8 servings

2 large ripe mangos
$^1/_3$ cup sugar (75 ml)

Combine in double boiler over medium heat. Cook 10 minutes. Purée and chill while preparing ice cream.

4 egg yolks
$^1/_2$ cup sugar (125 ml)
1 tsp vanilla (5 ml)
1 cup half and half (250 ml)

Whip ingredients until combined and place in a double boiler over medium heat. Beat until double in volume, 5-7 minutes. Take off heat and place in bowl of cold water until cool.

1 $^3/_4$ cups whipping cream (425 ml)

Add to egg mixture, blend and then pour into ice cream machine. Freeze according to manufacturer's instructions. When half-frozen, add mango purée and continue to freeze.

Assembly

Place 1 scoop ice cream into individual dishes. Top with thin slice of ripe mango and pour 1 tbsp (15 ml) of peach liqueur over top. Serve with fancy wafer.

Note:

Ice cream is best if taken out of freezer and placed in refrigerator half an hour before serving.

Index

BACK COVER CREDITS

Back Row, left to right
    Paul's French Foods – **Max Wirth**
    Baker Street – **Mary Somerton**
    Sutton Place – **Brian Morin**
    Bear Essentials — **Nancy Gangbar**
    Treats – **Elizabeth Volgyesi**
    King Edward Hotel – **Joel Gaillot**

Middle row, l. to r.
    Dessert Peddler – **Mary Ann Moran**
    W.D. Jones – **John Matheson**
    Baker Street – **Esther Kravice**
    Carole's Cheesecake Company – **Carole Ogus**
    L'Hôtel – **Philippe Egalon**
    Sweet Sue Pastries – **Sue Devor**

Front Row, l. to r.
    Patachou – **Christian Serebecbere**
    Inn of the Park – **Sitram Sharma**
    Author – **Rose Reisman**
    Fenton's – **Werner Bassen**
    Four Seasons Yorkville – **Wolfgang von Wieser**